FROM THE DEPTHS OF OUR HEARTS

BENEDICT XVI

ROBERT CARDINAL SARAH

From the Depths
of Our Hearts

Priesthood, Celibacy, and the
Crisis of the Catholic Church

Translated by Michael J. Miller

IGNATIUS PRESS   SAN FRANCISCO

Nicolas Diat edited this work for publication

Original French edition:
Des Profondeurs de nos cœurs
© 2020 Librairie Arthème Fayard, Paris

Cover photographs:
Photograph of Benedict XVI: © Stefano Spaziani
Photograph of Robert Cardinal Sarah: © Éric Vandeville

Cover design by John Herreid

© 2020 by Ignatius Press, San Francisco
All rights reserved
ISBN 978-1-62164-414-9 (HB)
ISBN 978-1-64229-119-3 (eBook)
Library of Congress Control Number 2020930631
Printed in Canada ∞

In tribute to the priests throughout the world.

Today, having a clear faith based on the Creed of the Church is often labeled as fundamentalism. Whereas relativism, that is, letting oneself be "tossed here and there, carried about by every wind of doctrine", seems the only attitude that can cope with modern times. We are building a dictatorship of relativism that does not recognize anything as definitive and whose ultimate goal consists solely of one's own ego and desires.

JOSEPH RATZINGER, homily given in the Basilica of Saint Peter on April 18, 2005

All activity must be preceded by an intense life of prayer, contemplation, seeking and listening to God's will.

ROBERT CARDINAL SARAH,
with NICOLAS DIAT,
The Power of Silence: Against the Dictatorship of Noise

CONTENTS

EDITOR'S NOTE

We must meditate on these reflections of a man
who is approaching the end of his life. At this
crucial hour, one does not take speech lightly.

ROBERT CARDINAL SARAH

From the Depths of Our Hearts: this is the simple,
moving title that Pope Emeritus Benedict XVI
and Robert Cardinal Sarah chose for the book
that they are publishing together.

Speech by Benedict XVI is rare. In March
2013, the pope emeritus wished to retire to a
monastery in the Vatican Gardens. He wanted
to dedicate the final years of his life to prayer,
meditation, and study. Silence became the sanctuary for a life far from the noise and the vio-
lence of the world. Until today, Benedict XVI
has rarely agreed to speak in order to express his
thought about important subjects in the life of
the Church.

The text that he is offering today is therefore exceptional. We are not talking about an

editorial or about notes collected over the years, but rather about an instructive reflection, *lectio* [lecture, exposition], and *disputatio* [disputation, debate] at the same time. The intention of Benedict XVI is clearly stated in his introduction: "Given the lasting crisis that the priesthood has been going through for many years, it seemed to me necessary to get to the deep roots of the problem."

Astute readers of the pope emeritus will have no difficulty recognizing the style, the logic, and the wonderful pedagogy of the author of the trilogy dedicated to Jesus of Nazareth. The discourse is structured, the citations are abundant, and the argumentation is polished.

Why did the pope emeritus wish to work with Cardinal Sarah? The two men are close friends. They keep up a regular correspondence in which they share their viewpoints, their hopes, and their fears.

In October 2019, the Synod on Amazonia— the assembly of bishops, men and women religious, and missionaries dedicated to the future of that immense region—was a time of discussion in the heart of the Church in which the future of the Catholic priesthood was addressed in various ways. For their part, from late summer of 2019 on, Benedict XVI and Cardinal Sarah exchanged texts, thoughts, and proposals. They met in order to bring greater clarity to the pages that are confided to the reader here.

I was privileged and dazzled to witness this dialogue. I cannot thank them enough for the honor given to me today to be the editor of this book.

The text by Benedict XVI is soberly entitled: "The Catholic Priesthood". Right away the pope emeritus explains his approach: "At the foundation of the serious situation in which the priesthood finds itself today, we find a methodological flaw in the reception of Scripture as Word of God." This is a severe, worrisome, almost unbelievable statement.

Benedict XVI did not want to address such a delicate problem alone. Cardinal Sarah's collaboration seemed to him natural and important. The pope emeritus is acquainted with the cardinal's deep spirituality, his sense of prayer, his wisdom. He has confidence in him. In the remarks he contributed to Cardinal Sarah's *The Power of Silence*, Benedict XVI wrote during Holy Week in the year 2017: "Cardinal Sarah is a spiritual teacher, who speaks out of the depths of silence with the Lord, out of his interior union with him, and thus really has something to say to each one of us. We should be grateful to Pope Francis for appointing such a spiritual teacher as head of the congregation that is responsible for the celebration of the liturgy in the Church."[1]

For his part, Cardinal Sarah admires the theological work of Benedict XVI, the power of his reflection, his humility and charity.

The intention of the authors is expressed perfectly in this sentence from their joint introduction to the book: "The similarity of our concerns and the convergence of our conclusions persuaded us to place the fruit of our work and of our spiritual friendship at the disposal of all the faithful, following the example of Saint Augustine."

The situation is simple. Two bishops decided to reflect. Two bishops decided to make public the fruit of their eminent research. The text by Benedict XVI is of high theological caliber. The one by Cardinal Sarah has a formidable catechetical strength. Their arguments intersect, their words complement each other, their intellects are mutually stimulating.

Cardinal Sarah chose as the title of his letter: "Loving to the End: An Ecclesiological and Pastoral Look at Priestly Celibacy". In it we find

---

[1] Cardinal Robert Sarah, with Nicolas Diat, *The Power of Silence: Against the Dictatorship of Noise*, trans. Michael J. Miller (San Francisco: Ignatius Press, 2017), 244.

again the courage, the radical approach, and the mysticism that make all his books so ardent.

Benedict XVI and Cardinal Sarah wished to open and close this book with two joint texts. In their conclusion they write: "It is urgent and necessary for everyone—bishops, priests, and lay people—to stop letting themselves be intimidated by the wrong-headed pleas, the theatrical productions, the diabolical lies, and the fashionable errors that try to devalue priestly celibacy."

Obviously the pope emeritus and Cardinal Sarah did not want to hide any of the anxiety that grips their hearts. But they are too well acquainted with Saint Augustine, to whom they turn frequently, not to know that love always has the last word.

Joseph Cardinal Ratzinger's episcopal motto was: "*Cooperatores Veritatis*": We must serve in such a way that we might be "coworkers with the truth". In this essay, at the age of ninety-two, he wished again to serve the truth. Cardinal Sarah's motto, chosen when he was the young archbishop of Conakry, the capital of Guinea, is: "*Sufficit tibi gratia mea*": "My grace is sufficient for you." It was taken from the Second Letter to the Corinthians, in which the Apostle Paul describes his doubts, fearing that he will not be capable of transmitting the teaching of the Gospel effectively. But God answers him: "My grace is sufficient for you, for my power is made perfect in weakness" (2 Cor 12:9).

I would like to conclude these remarks with two quotations that resound forcefully today. The first is drawn from the homily of Benedict XVI for the Mass on Pentecost, May 31, 2009: "Just as an atmospheric pollution exists that poisons the environment and living beings, thus a pollution of heart and spirit exists that mortifies and poisons spiritual life." The second is taken from *The Portal of the Mystery of Hope* by Charles Péguy: "What surprises me, says God, is hope. And I can't get over it. This little hope who seems like nothing at all. This little girl hope."[2]

In searching the depths of their hearts, Benedict XVI and Robert Cardinal Sarah tried to dispel this pollution and to open the doors of hope.

Nicolas Diat
Rome, December 6, 2019

---

[2] Charles Péguy, *The Portal of the Mystery of Hope*, trans. David Louis Schindler, Jr. (Grand Rapids, Mich.: Eerdmans, collection 1996), 7.

What Do You Fear?

Introduction by the Two Authors

In a famous letter addressed to the Donatist bishop Maximin, Saint Augustine announces his intention to publish his correspondence. "What shall I do," he asks, "but read our letters to the Catholic people, in order that they may be better instructed?"[1] We have decided to follow the example of the bishop of Hippo.

In recent months, while the world was echoing with the din created by a strange media synod that overrode the real synod, we met together. We exchanged our ideas and our anxieties. We prayed and meditated in silence. Each of our meetings mutually strengthened and calmed us. Our reflections, conducted along different lines, led us to exchange letters. The similarity of our concerns and the convergence of our conclusions persuaded us to place the fruit of our work and of our spiritual friendship at the disposal of all the faithful, following the example of Saint Augustine.

Indeed, like him we can declare: "*Silere non possum!* I cannot be silent ... for I know how

[1] Saint Augustine, *Letter* 23, 6, in *The Works of Saint Augustine*, vol. II/1, *Letters 1–99* (Charlottesville, Va.: New City Press, 2000), pp. 63–68 at 67.

dangerous for me such silence is. After all, I do not plan to pass my time in the vanity of ecclesiastical honors; rather, I bear in mind that I will give an account to the prince of all pastors [Christ] about the sheep entrusted to me. I cannot be silent and pretend nothing is wrong."[2]

As bishops, we are responsible for the care of all the Churches. In our great desire for peace and unity, we therefore offer to all our brother bishops, priests, and the lay faithful throughout the world the benefit of our exchanges.

We do this in a spirit of love for the Church's unity. Although ideology divides, truth unites hearts. Scrutinizing the doctrine of salvation can only unite the Church around her Divine Master.

We do this in a spirit of charity. To us it appeared useful and necessary to publish this work at a time when minds seem to have calmed down. Everyone can complete it or critique it. The search for truth can be made only by opening the heart.

Therefore we fraternally offer these reflections to the people of God and, of course, in a spirit of filial obedience, to Pope Francis.

We thought in particular about the priests. Our priestly hearts wished to strengthen them, to

---

[2] Ibid., 67.

encourage them. With all priests, we pray: Save us, Lord, for we are perishing! The Lord is asleep while the storm is unleashed. He seems to abandon us to the waves of doubt and error. We are tempted to lose confidence. On every side, the waves of relativism are submerging the barque of the Church. The apostles were afraid. Their faith had grown lukewarm. The Church, too, sometimes seems to be unsteady. In the midst of the storm, the apostles' confidence in Jesus' power was shaken. We are experiencing this same mystery. Nevertheless, we are at peace, for we know that Jesus is the one steering the ship. We know that it will never sink. We know that it alone can bring us to the port of eternal salvation.

We know that Jesus is here, with us, in the ship. We want to declare to him again our confidence and our absolute, full, and undivided fidelity. We want to say to him again the great "Yes" that we said to him on the day of our ordination. Our priestly celibacy causes us to live out this total "Yes" each day. For our celibacy is a proclamation of faith. It is a testimony, because it causes us to enter into a life that makes sense only in terms of God. Our celibacy is a witness, in other words, a martyrdom. The Greek word has both meanings. In the storm, we priests must reaffirm that we are ready to lose our lives for Christ. Day after day, we give this witness thanks to the celibacy through which we give away our lives.

Jesus is asleep in the barque. But if hesitation gains the upper hand, if we are afraid of putting our trust in him, if celibacy makes us turn back, then we fear that we will hear his reproach: "Why are you afraid, O men of little faith?" (Mt 8:26).

Text written by Cardinal Sarah,
read and approved by Benedict XVI.
Vatican City, September, 2019

I

The Catholic Priesthood

by Benedict XVI

Given the lasting crisis that the priesthood has been going through for many years, it seemed to me necessary to get to the deep roots of the problem. I had started a work of theological reflection, but age and a kind of weariness led me to abandon it. My exchanges with Robert Cardinal Sarah gave me the strength to resume it and to bring it to completion.

At the foundation of the serious situation in which the priesthood finds itself today, we find a methodological flaw in the reception of Scripture as Word of God.

The abandonment of the Christological interpretation of the Old Testament led many contemporary exegetes to a deficient theology of worship. They did not understand that Jesus, far from abolishing the worship and adoration owed to God, took them upon himself and accomplished them in the loving act of his sacrifice. As a result, some went so far as to reject the necessity of an authentically cultic priesthood in the New Covenant.

In the first part of my study, I have tried to bring to light the fundamental exegetical structure that allows a correct theology of the priesthood.

In the second part, by applying this hermeneutic to the study of three texts, I have spelled out the requirements of worship in spirit and in truth. From now on, the cultic act proceeds by way of an offering of the totality of one's life in love. The priesthood of Jesus Christ causes us to enter into a life that consists of becoming one with him and renouncing all that belongs only to us. For priests, this is the foundation of the necessity of celibacy but also of liturgical prayer, meditation on the Word of God, and the renunciation of material goods.

I thank dear Cardinal Sarah for having given me the opportunity to savor anew the taste of the texts from the Word of God that have guided my steps every day of my life as a priest.

The elaboration of the New Testament priesthood in Christological-Pneumatological exegesis

The movement that had formed around Jesus of Nazareth was a movement of laymen—at least during the pre-Paschal period. In this respect, it resembled the movement of the Pharisees, and this is why the first conflicts described in the Gospels refer essentially to the latter. Only at the time of the last *Pesach* [Passover] of Jesus in Jerusalem did the priestly aristocracy of the Temple—the Sadducees—notice Jesus and his movement, which led to the trial, the condemnation, and the execution of Jesus. The Temple priesthood was hereditary: a man who was not descended from a family of priests could not become a priest. Consequently, the ministries of the community that started to form around Jesus could not be part of the framework of the Old Testament priesthood.

Let us examine quickly the essential ministerial structures of the first community of Jesus.

Apostolos

In the Greek world, the word "apostle" is a technical term that belongs to the language of political institutions.[1] In pre-Christian Judaism, this word is used to interconnect the secular function of an envoy, responsibility to God, and religious significance. In this context, it designates an envoy authorized by God and appointed for a task.

Episkopos

In Greek, in everyday language, the word *episkopos* indicates functions associated with tasks of a

---

[1] Cf. Gerhard Kittel and Friedrich Gerhard, eds., *Theologisches Wörterbuch zum Neuen Testament* (1933; Stuttgart: Kohlhammer, 1957–1979), 1:406.

technical and financial nature. However, it also has a religious sense, inasmuch as the ones who are called *episkopos*, that is, "protector", are most often the gods. "The Septuagint uses the word *episkopos* in the two senses already in use in the pagan Greek world: on the one hand, as a name of God and, on the other hand, in the profane and generic sense of 'overseer'."[2]

Presbyteros

While among the Christians of Gentile origin, the term *episkopos* is most often used to refer to ministers, the word *presbyteros* is characteristic of the Judeo-Christian milieu. In Jerusalem, the Jewish tradition of the "elder", considered as a sort of institutional organ, developed rapidly, to the point of becoming an initial form of Christian ministry.

From that moment on, the Church composed of Jews and Gentiles showed the development of the threefold form of ministry composed of bishops, priests, and deacons. We find it already clearly mentioned by Ignatius of Antioch in the late first century. To this day, it has expressed appropriately the ministerial structure of the Church of Jesus Christ both terminologically and ontologically.

[2] Ibid., 2:610.

We must draw an initial conclusion from the preceding remarks. The lay character of Jesus' first movement and the non-cultic, non-priestly character of the first ministries do not proceed from an anti-cultic and anti-Jewish choice. They are a consequence of the particular situation of the priesthood of the Old Testament, in which the priesthood is reserved exclusively to the tribe of Aaron-Levi. In the two other "lay movements" at the time of Jesus, the relation with the priesthood is different: the Pharisees seem to have lived basically in harmony with the Temple hierarchy, while opposing it on the subject of belief in the resurrection of the body. Among the Essenes and the movement revealed by the Qumran manuscripts, which seems to be connected with it, the situation is more complex. One part of the Qumran movement was marked by its opposition to the Herodian Temple and to the priesthood that corresponded to it. It was a matter, not of denying the priesthood, but rather of reconstituting it in its pure, correct form. Similarly, in Jesus' movement, it is absolutely not a question of "desacralization", "delegalization", or a rejection of the priesthood and the hierarchy. The prophets' critique of worship is certainly assumed, but it is unified in a surprising way with the priestly and cultic tradition in a synthesis that we must attempt to understand. In my book *The Spirit of* the *Liturgy*,[3] I explained the different critiques of the prophets concerning worship. They were taken up again by Stephen, and Saint Paul links them with the new cultic tradition of Jesus' Last Supper. Jesus himself had repeated and approved the prophets' critique of worship, in particular on the subject of the difference of opinion concerning the correct interpretation of the *Shabbat* (cf. Mt 12:7–8).

Let us examine first Jesus' relation with the Temple as the expression of God's special presence in the midst of his chosen people and as the place of worship for which Moses had set the rules. The episode of the twelve-year-old Jesus in the Temple shows that his family was observant and that he himself participated in the devotion of his own family. The words that he addressed to his mother: "Did you not know that I must be in my Father's house?" (Lk 2:49) express the conviction that the Temple represents in a special way the place where God dwells and, therefore, the appropriate place for the Son to live. Similarly, during the short period of his public life, Jesus participated in Israel's pilgrimages to the Temple, and, after his Resurrection, it is well known that his community met regularly in the Temple for teaching and prayers.

---

[3] Joseph Ratzinger, *The Spirit of the Liturgy*, with *The Spirit of the Liturgy*, by Romano Guardini (San Francisco: Ignatius Press, 2018).

And yet, through the cleansing of the Temple, Jesus intended to introduce a fundamentally new emphasis (Mk 11:15ff.; Jn 2:13–22). The interpretation whereby the sole intention of this gesture of Jesus was to combat abuses and thus to confirm the function of the Temple is inadequate. In John, we find words that interpret Jesus' action as a prefiguration of the destruction of this building of stone, which was to be replaced by his own body as the new Temple. In the Synoptic Gospels, this interpretation of Jesus appears on the lips of false witnesses at his trial (Mk 14:58). The witnesses' version was distorted, and therefore it could not be used within the context of the trial. But the fact remains that Jesus had indeed made these statements, the actual wording of which could not be determined with sufficient certainty during the trial. The nascent Church was therefore correct to assume that the Johannine version was authentically from Jesus. This means that Jesus considers the destruction of the Temple as the consequence of the erroneous attitude of the highest authorities of the priestly hierarchy. Nevertheless, as at every crucial moment in salvation history, God utilizes here the erroneous behavior of men as a *modus* [means] of manifesting a greater love. In the final analysis, Jesus considers the destruction of the existing Temple as a stage in the divine healing. He interprets it as the formation and organization of a new and definitive worship. In this sense, the cleansing of the Temple is the announcement of a new form of divine adoration, and consequently it concerns the nature of worship and of the priesthood.

It is obvious that the Last Supper, with the offering of the Body and Blood of Jesus Christ, is decisive for an understanding of what Jesus intended or rejected on the subject of worship. There is no room here to enter into the controversy that developed later over the exact interpretation of this event and of Jesus' words. On the other hand, it is important to emphasize that Jesus adopts the tradition of Sinai and thus presents himself as the new Moses, but also the hope of the New Covenant, which was formulated in a particular way by Jeremiah. He thus announces a development beyond the Sinai tradition, at the center of which he himself stands as both the one sacrificing and as the victim. It is indeed necessary to consider that this Jesus who stands in the midst of his disciples is also the one who gives himself to them in his flesh and in his blood, thus anticipating the Cross and the Resurrection. Without the Resurrection, all this would have no meaning. The crucifixion of Jesus is not in itself a cultic act. The Roman soldiers who execute him are not priests. They set about putting a man to death; they have absolutely no thought of performing an act pertaining to worship. The fact that Jesus gives himself forever as food during the Last Supper signifies the anticipation of his death and Resurrection. This signifies the transformation of an act of human cruelty into an act of love and self-giving. So it is that Jesus accomplishes the fundamental renewal of worship that will forever remain valid and obligatory. He transforms the sin of men into an act of forgiveness and love into which his future disciples can enter by participating in what Jesus instituted. Thus we understand what Saint Augustine calls, in the Church, the transition from the Last Supper to the morning sacrifice. The Last Supper is the gift that God grants us in the love of Jesus who forgives. Humanity in turn can receive this gesture of love from God and return it to God.

In all this, it is never directly a question of priesthood. However, it is clearly evident that the former order of Aaron is outmoded and that Jesus himself appears as the High Priest. In Jesus, the cultic tradition that goes back to Moses merges with the critique of worship by the prophets. Love and sacrifice are one. In my book on Jesus,[4] I explained how this new foundation of worship

---

[4] Joseph Ratzinger/Benedict XVI, *Jesus of Nazareth*, vol. 2, *From the Entrance into Jerusalem to the Resurrection*, trans. Philip J. Whitmore (San Francisco: Ignatius Press, 2011), 38–41.

and, with it, of the priesthood is already completely accomplished in Saint Paul. This fundamental unity between love and sacrifice is based
on the mediation established by the death and
Resurrection of Jesus. It was clearly admitted even
by the adversaries of Paul's proclamation.

The destruction of the Temple walls, caused by
man, is accepted in a positive way by God. There
are no more walls, because the Risen Christ has
become, for mankind, the space in which to adore
God. In this way, the collapse of the Herodian
Temple signifies that now nothing more comes
between, on the one hand, the linguistic and existential space of the Mosaic legislation and, on the
other hand, the space of the movement gathered
around Jesus. The Christian ministries (*episkopos,
presbyteros, diakonos*) and those that were regulated
by the Mosaic law (high priests, priests, Levites)
from now on stand openly side by side. The former can now be identified in relation to the others in a new clarity. Indeed, the terminological
equivalence comes about rather quickly: *episkopos*
designates the High Priest, *presbyteros* the priest,
diakonos the Levite. We find it very clearly in the
catecheses on Baptism by Saint Ambrose, who
is certainly referring to older models and docu-
ments, to which Saint Clement of Rome is one of
the first witnesses, around the year 96, in his *First
Letter to the Corinthians*:

We are obliged to carry out in fullest detail what the Master commanded us to do at stated times. He has ordered the sacrifices to be offered and the services to be held, and this not in a random or irregular fashion, but at definite times and seasons.... Special functions are assigned to the high priest; a special office is imposed upon the priests; and special ministrations fall to the Levites. The layman is bound by the rules laid down for the laity.[5]

Thus we are witnessing the emergence of the Christological interpretation of the Old Testament, which can also be considered a Pneumatological interpretation. This is how the Old Testament was able to become and to remain the Bible of the Christians. This Christological-Pneumatological interpretation was described as "allegorical" from a historical-literary perspective. But it is obvious that we must read [i.e., discern] in it the reason for the profound novelty of the Christian interpretation of the Old Testament. Here allegory is not a literary means of making the text applicable to new purposes. It is the expression of a historical transition that corresponds to the internal logic of the text.

[5] Clement of Rome, *First Epistle of Clement to the Corinthians*, XL, 1–5, in *The Epistles of St. Clement of Rome and St. Ignatius of Antioch*, trans. James A. Kleist, ACW 1 (Westminster, Md.: Newman Bookshop, 1946), 33–34.

The Cross of Jesus Christ is the act of radical love in which reconciliation really is accomplished between God and the world marred by sin. This is the reason why this event, which in itself is not of a cultic type, represents the supreme adoration of God. In the Cross, the "katabatic" line of descent from God and the "anabatic" line of humanity's offering to God become a single act. Through the Cross, the Body of Christ becomes the new Temple at the time of the Resurrection. In the celebration of the Eucharist, the Church and even humanity are ceaselessly drawn into this process and involved in it. In the Cross of Christ, the critique of worship by the prophets definitively reaches its goal. Even so, a new worship is instituted at the same time. The love of Christ, which is always present in the Eucharist, is the new act of adoration. Consequently, the priestly ministries of Israel are "annulled" in the service of love, which always signifies concomitantly the adoration of God. This new unity of love and worship, of critique of worship and glorification of God in the service of love, is certainly an unprecedented task that has been entrusted to the Church and that each generation must accomplish anew.

Thus, the pneumatic development beyond the Old Testament "letter" in the ministry of the New Covenant always requires new developments beyond the "letter" in the spirit. In the sixteenth century, Luther, who based his teaching on a completely different reading of the Old Testament, was no longer in a position to make this transition. For this reason, he interpreted Old Testament worship and the priesthood that was designed for it solely as an expression of the "law". Now, for him, the law was not a path of God's grace but was opposed to it. He was therefore compelled to set up a radical opposition between the New Testament ministerial offices and the priesthood as such.

At the time of Vatican II, this question of the opposition between ministries and priesthood became absolutely unavoidable for the Catholic Church as well. Indeed, "allegory" as a pneumatic transition from the Old to the New Testament had become incomprehensible. The decree of the council on the ministry and life of priests hardly deals with this question at all. Nevertheless, in the period that followed, it monopolized our attention with an unprecedented urgency, and it turned into a crisis of the priesthood that has lasted to this day in the Church.

I would like to illustrate this statement by mentioning two personal observations. The manner in which one of my friends, the great India expert Paul Hacker, confronted this question with his customary passion in his conversion from staunch Lutheranism to Catholicism, has remained engraved on my memory. He considered "priests" to be a definitively outmoded reality in the New Testament. With passionate indignation, he was opposed above all to the fact that in the German word *Priester*, which comes from the Greek *presbyteros*, the connotation of *sacerdotium* [Latin: priesthood] continued to resonate in spite of everything—and this is true. I no longer know how he finally succeeded in resolving this question.

I myself, during a conference on priesthood in the Church that was held immediately after the council, thought that I had to present the priest of the New Testament as the one who meditates on the Word, and not as a "craftsman of worship". It is true that meditation on the Word of God is an important and fundamental task of the priest of God in the New Covenant. Even so, this Word was made flesh. To meditate on it always means also to be nourished by the flesh that is given to us in the Most Holy Eucharist as bread from heaven. To meditate on the Word in the Church of the New Covenant always amounts to abandoning oneself to the flesh of Jesus Christ. This abandonment implies accepting our own transformation by the Cross.

I will return to this subject farther on. For the moment, let us examine several stages in the concrete development of the history of the Church.

We can observe a first step in the institution of a new ministry. The Acts of the Apostles mention the excess workload of the apostles, who, in addition to their task of preaching and of leading the Church's prayer, had to take upon themselves at the same time full responsibility for the care of the poor. One result of this was that the Hellenistic part of the nascent Church felt neglected. The apostles then decided to devote themselves entirely to prayer and the service of the Word. For charitable works, they created the ministry of the Seven, which was later identified with the diaconate. Moreover, the example of Saint Stephen shows that this ministry, too, required not only purely practical work of a charitable nature, but also the Spirit and faith and, therefore, the ability to serve the Word.

One problem, which has remained crucial to this day, emerged from the fact that the new ministries were based, not on familial descent, but on divine election and vocation. Formerly, the continuity of the priestly hierarchy of Israel was assured by God himself, since, in the final analysis, he was the one who gave children to parents. The new ministries, on the other hand, were based, not on membership in a family, but on a vocation given by God. Furthermore, this call must be recognized and accepted by the man to whom it is addressed. This is why, in the New Testament community, the problem of vocations arises from the very beginning: "Pray therefore the Lord of the harvest to send out laborers into his harvest" (Mt 9:38). In every generation, the Church is moved by the hope and concern of finding those who are called. We know how great a labor and a worry this question still is for the Church.

There is another question that is directly connected with this problem. Very quickly—we do not know exactly when, but in any case very rapidly—the regular and even daily celebration of the Eucharist became essential for the Church. The "supersubstantial" bread is at the same time the "daily" bread of the Church. This had an important consequence, which is precisely what haunts the Church today.[6]

In the common awareness of Israel, priests were strictly obliged to observe sexual abstinence during the times when they led worship and were therefore in contact with the divine mystery. The relation between sexual abstinence and divine worship was absolutely clear in the common

---

[6] On the topic of the meaning of the word *epioúsios (supersubstantialis)*, see Eckhard Nordhofen, "What Bread Is This? What Bread This Is!", *International Catholic Review Communio* 44/1 (2017): 43–71; Gerd Neuhaus, "Möglichkeit und Grenzen einer Gottespräsenz im menschlichen 'Fleisch': Anmerkungen zu Eckhard Nordhofens Relektüre der vierten Vaterunser-Bitte" [Possibility and limits of a divine presence in human 'flesh'; Remarks on Eckhard Nordhofen's rereading of the fourth petition of the Our Father], *Internazionale katholische Zeitschrift Communio* 46/1 (2017): 23–32.

awareness of Israel. By way of example, I wish to recall the episode about David, who, while fleeing Saul, asked the priest Ahimelech to give him some bread: "The priest answered David, 'I have no common bread at hand, but there is holy bread; if only the young men have kept themselves from women.' And David answered the priest, 'Of a truth women have been kept from us as always when I go on an expedition'" (1 Sam 21:4–5). Since the priests of the Old Testament had to dedicate themselves to worship only during set times, marriage and the priesthood were compatible.

But because of the regular and often even daily celebration of the Eucharist, the situation of the priests of the Church of Jesus Christ has changed radically. From now on, their entire life is in contact with the divine mystery. This requires on their part exclusivity with regard to God. Consequently, this excludes other ties that, like marriage, involve one's whole life. From the daily celebration of the Eucharist, which implies a permanent state of service to God, was born spontaneously the impossibility of a matrimonial bond. We can say that the sexual abstinence that was functional was transformed automatically into an ontological abstinence. Thus, its motivation and its significance were changed from within and profoundly.

Nowadays some scholars too readily make the facile statement that all this was just the result of a contempt for corporeality and sexuality. The critique claiming that priestly celibacy was founded on a Manichaean concept of the world was formulated as early as the fourth century. This critique was immediately rejected, however, in a decisive way by the Fathers of the Church, who put an end to it for a certain time.

Such a judgment [of consecrated celibacy] is wrong. To prove this, it is enough to recall that the Church has always considered marriage as a gift granted by God ever since the earthly paradise. However, the married state involves a man in his totality, and since serving the Lord likewise requires the total gift of a man, it does not seem possible to carry on the two vocations simultaneously. Thus, the ability to renounce marriage so as to place oneself totally at the Lord's disposition became a criterion for priestly ministry.

As for the concrete form of celibacy in the early Church, it is advisable also to emphasize that married men could not receive the sacrament of Holy Orders unless they had pledged to observe sexual abstinence, therefore, to live in a so-called "Josephite" marriage, like the marriage of Saint Joseph and the Virgin Mary. Such a situation seems to have been altogether normal over the course of the first centuries. There were a sufficient number of men and women who considered it reasonable and possible to live in this way while together dedicating themselves to the Lord.[7]

Three texts that clarify the Christian notion of priesthood

To complete these reflections, I would like to interpret three texts from Sacred Scripture that reveal the profound unity between the two Testaments through the transition from the Temple of stone to the Temple which is the Body of Christ. However, this unity is not simply mechanical; it results from progress that shows how thoroughly the profound intention of the initial words is accomplished precisely by the transition from the "letter" to the Spirit.

Psalm 16:5–6: the words used for admission to the clerical state before the council

First I would like to interpret the words of verses 5 and 6 of Psalm 16, which, before Vatican Council

---

[7] The reader can find extensive information on the history of celibacy in the first centuries in Stefan Heid, *Celibacy in the Early Church: The Beginnings of a Discipline of Obligatory Continence for Clerics in East and West*, trans. Michael J. Miller (San Francisco: Ignatius Press, 2000; original German edition 1997).

II, were used during the tonsure ceremony that
marked entrance into the clergy. These words
were recited by the bishop, then repeated by the
candidate, who in this way was welcomed into
the clergy of the Church: "*Dominus pars hereditatis
meae et calicis mei; tu es qui restitues hereditatem meam
mihi*": "The LORD is my chosen portion and my
cup; you hold my lot. The lines have fallen for me
in pleasant places; yes, I have a goodly heritage"
(Ps 16:5–6). Indeed, the psalm expresses exactly,
in the Old Testament, what it signifies later on in
the Church: acceptance into the priestly community. This passage recalls that all the tribes of Israel,
as well as each family, represented the heritage of
God's promise to Abraham. This was expressed
concretely in the fact that each family obtained as
its inheritance a portion of the Promised Land, of
which it became the owner. Possession of a part
of the Holy Land gave to each family the certainty
that it was sharing in the promise. In concrete
terms, it assured them a livelihood. Each man
had to obtain as much land as he needed in order
to live. The story of Naboth (1 Kings 21:1–29),
who absolutely refused to give his vineyard away
to King Ahab, even though the latter said that he
was willing to reimburse him completely, clearly
shows the importance of this concrete share of
the heritage. For Naboth, the vineyard was more
than a valuable plot of land: it was his share in

the promise that God made to Israel. Whereas each Israelite had at his disposal a tract of land that assured him of what he needed in order to live, the tribe of Levi had a peculiar feature: it was the only tribe that did not possess land as its heritage. The Levite remained without land and was therefore deprived of an immediate subsistence derived from the land. He lived only by God and for God. In practice, this implies that he had to live, according to precise norms, on the sacrificial offerings that Israel set aside for God.

This Old Testament prefiguration is fulfilled in the priests of the Church in a new and deeper way: they must live only by God and for him. Saint Paul clearly spells out what this implies concretely. The apostle lives on what people give him, because he himself gives them the Word of God that is our authentic bread and our true life. In the Old Testament, the Levites renounce the possession of land. In the New Testament, this privation is transformed and renewed: priests, because they are radically consecrated to God, renounce marriage and family. The Church interpreted the word "clergy" in this sense. To enter the clergy means to renounce a self-centered life and to accept God alone as the support and guarantee of one's own life.

The true foundation of the life of a priest, the salt of his existence, the earth or "land" of his life, is God himself. Celibacy, which applies to bishops throughout the Church, in both East and West, and, according to a tradition going back to a time close to that of the apostles, to priests in general in the Latin Church, can be understood and experienced definitively only on this foundation.

I had meditated for a long time on this idea during the retreat that I had preached in Lent 1983 for John Paul II and the Roman Curia:

> There is no need to make any great transposition [of the psalm] in our own [priestly] spiritual life. Fundamental parts of the priesthood are something like the status of the Levites, exposed, not having land, wholy dependent on God. The account of vocation in Luke 5,1–11, which we considered first, ends not without reason with the words: "They left everything and followed him" (v. 11). Without such a forsaking on our part there is no priesthood. The call to follow is not possible without this sign of freedom and renunciation of any kind of compromise. I think that from this point of view celibacy acquires its great significance as a forgoing of a future earthly home and the leading of one's own life in chosen and familiar surroundings, and that thus it becomes truly indispensable, in order that being given over to God may remain fundamental and become truly realized. This means—it is clear—that celibacy imposes its demands in whatever setting up of one's life. Its full significance cannot be attained if for everything else we follow

the rules of property and of life's game as commonly accepted today. It is above all not possible for celibacy to have stability if we do not make remaining close to God the center of our life.

Psalm 16, like Psalm 119, is a strong pointer to the necessity for continual meditation to make the word of God our own, for only so can we become at home with it and can it become our home. The community aspect of liturgical prayer and worship necessarily connected with this comes out here, where Psalm 16 speaks of the Lord as 'my cup' (v. 5). In accordance with the language usual in the Old Testament this reference is to the festive cup which would have been passed round from hand to hand at the sacrificial meal, or to the fatal cup, the cup of wrath or salvation. The New Testament priest who prays the psalm can find indicated here in a special way that chalice by means of which the Lord in the deepest sense has become our land, our inheritance: the Eucharistic Chalice, in which he shares himself with us as our life. The priestly life in the presence of God thus takes on actuality in our life in virtue of the Eucharistic mystery. In the most profound sense, the Eucharist is the land which has become our portion and of which we can say: "The lines have fallen for me in pleasant places; yea, I have a goodly heritage" (v. 6).[8]

---

[8] Joseph Cardinal Ratzinger, *Journey to Easter*, trans. Dame Mary Groves (1987; New York: Crossroad, 2005), 154–55, lightly emended.

I still have a vivid memory of the day when, on the eve of receiving the tonsure, I meditated on this verse of Psalm 16. I suddenly understood what the Lord expected of me at that moment: he wanted to have my life completely at his disposal, and, at the same time, he entrusted himself entirely to me. Thus I could consider that the words of this psalm applied to my whole destiny: "The LORD is my chosen portion and my cup; you hold my lot. The lines have fallen for me in pleasant places; yes, I have a goodly heritage" (Ps 16:5–6).

The Book of Deuteronomy (10:8 and 18:5–8). The words incorporated into Eucharistic Prayer II: the role of the tribe of Levi reinterpreted from a Christological and Pneumatological perspective for the priests of the Church

Secondly, I would like to analyze a passage taken from Eucharistic Prayer II of the Roman Liturgy after the reform of Vatican Council II. The text of Eucharistic Prayer II is generally attributed to Saint Hippolytus (died around 235). In any case, it is very old. In it we find the following words: "Domine, panem vitae et calicem salutis offerimus, gratias agentes quia nos dignos habuisti astare coram te et tibi ministrare." [We offer you, Lord, the Bread of life and the Chalice of salvation, giving thanks that you have held us worthy to be in your presence and minister to you.] This sentence does not mean, as some liturgists would have us believe, that even during the Eucharist Prayer the priests and the faithful ought to stand and not kneel.[9] We can deduce the correct understanding of this sentence if we consider that it is taken literally from Deuteronomy 10:8 and from Deuteronomy 18:5–8, where the essential cultic role of the tribe of Levi is mentioned: "At that time the LORD set apart the tribe of Levi to carry the ark of the covenant of the LORD, to stand before the LORD to minister to him and to bless in his name" (Deut 10:8). "For the LORD your God has chosen him out of all your tribes, to stand and minister in the name of the LORD, him and his sons for ever" (Deut 18:5).

In Deuteronomy, the words "stand before God and serve him" serve to define the essence of the priesthood. They were later incorporated into

---

[9] While the official German translation of Eucharistic Prayer II says correctly: "... to stand before you and minister to you", the Italian translation simplifies the text by omitting the image of standing in God's presence. Indeed, it says: "Ti rendiamo grazie di averci ammessi alla tua presenza a compiere il servizio sacerdotale" (We give you thanks for having admitted us into your presence to perform the priestly service). [The English translation, as given in the third edition of the Roman Missal (2011), makes a similar simplification, substituting "be in your presence" for the word "stand", as seen above.]

the Eucharistic Prayer of the Church of Jesus
Christ to express the continuity and the newness
of the priesthood in the New Covenant. What
was said formerly about the tribe of Levi and con-
cerned it exclusively applies now to the priests
and the bishops of the Church. Based on a notion
inspired by the Reformation, one might be
tempted to say that we are looking here at a step
backward in relation to the newness of the community of Jesus Christ. One would be tempted to
see in it a relapse into a cultic priesthood that was
outmoded and should be rejected. Quite the contrary, it is precisely the step forward of the New
Covenant, which takes up into itself and at the
same time transforms the Old Covenant by ele-
vating it to the height of Jesus Christ. Priesthood
is no longer linked with membership in a family;
rather, it is open to humanity on a vast scale. It no
longer coincides with the administration of the
sacrifice in the Temple; rather it gathers humanity
in the love of Jesus Christ, which embraces the
whole world. Worship and the critique of worship, liturgical sacrifice and the service of love for
neighbor are now one. Consequently, the words
"astare coram te et tibi ministrare" ["to be in your
presence and minister to you"] do not envisage
an exterior attitude. On the contrary, they represent a profound point of unity between the Old
and the New Testament, and they describe the

very nature of the priesthood. In the final analysis, these words remind us of the fact that we all stand before God.

I tried to interpret this text in a homily given in Saint Peter's in Rome on Holy Thursday 2008; I cite here an excerpt from it:

At the same time Holy Thursday is an occasion for us to ask ourselves over and over again: to what did we say our "yes"? What does this "being a priest of Jesus Christ" mean? The Second Canon of our Missal, which was probably compiled in Rome already at the end of the second century, describes the essence of the priestly ministry with the words with which, in the *Book of Deuteronomy* (18:5–7), the essence of the Old Testament priesthood is described: *astare coram te et tibi ministrare* ["to stand and minister in the name of the Lord"]. There are therefore two duties that define the essence of the priestly ministry: in the first place, "to stand in the Lord's presence". In the *Book of Deuteronomy* this is read in the context of the preceding [regulation], according to which priests do not receive any portion of land in the Holy Land—they live of God and for God. They did not attend to the usual work necessary to sustain daily life. Their profession was to "stand in the Lord's presence"—to look to him, to be there for him. Hence, ultimately, the word indicated a life in God's presence, and with this also a ministry of representing others. As the others cultivated the land, from which the priest also lived, so he kept the world open to God, he had to live with his gaze on him.

Now if this word is found in the Canon of the Mass immediately after the consecration of the gifts, after the entrance of the Lord in the assembly of prayer, then for us this points to being before the Lord present, that is, it indicates the Eucharist as the center of priestly life. But here too, the meaning is deeper. During Lent the hymn that introduces the Office of Readings of the Liturgy of the Hours—the Office that monks once recited during the night vigil before God and for humanity—one of the duties of Lent is described with the imperative: *arctius perstemus in custodia*—we must be even more intensely alert. In the tradition of Syrian monasticism, monks were described as "those who remained standing". This standing was an expression of vigilance. What was considered here as a duty of the monks, we can rightly see also as an expression of the priestly mission and as a correct interpretation of the word of Deuteronomy: the priest must be on the watch. He must be on his guard in the face of the menacing powers of evil. He must keep the world awake for God. He must be the one who remains standing: upright before the trends of time. Upright in truth. Upright in the commitment for good. Standing before the Lord must always also include, at its depths, responsibility for humanity to the Lord, who in his turn takes on the burden of all of us to the Father. And it must be a taking on of him, of Christ, of his word, his truth, his love. The priest must be upright, fearless and prepared to sustain even insults for the Lord, as referred to in the *Acts of the Apostles*: they were "rejoicing that they were counted worthy to suffer dishonor for the name" of Jesus (5:41).

Now let us move on to the second word that the Second Canon repeats from the Old Testament text—"to stand in your presence and serve you". The priest must be an upright person, vigilant, a person who remains standing. Service is then added to all this. In the Old Testament text this word has an essentially ritualistic meaning: all acts of worship foreseen by the Law are the priests' duty. But this action, according to the rite, was classified as service, as a duty of service, and thus it explains in what spirit this activity was supposed to take place. With the use of the word "serve" in the Canon, the liturgical meaning of this term was adopted in a certain way—in keeping with the novelty of the Christian cult. What the priest does at that moment, in the Eucharistic celebration, is to serve God and men. The cult that Christ rendered to the Father was the giving of himself to the end for humanity. Into this cult, this service, the priest must insert himself. Thus, the word "serve" contains many dimensions. In the first place,

part of it is certainly the correct celebration of
the liturgy and of the sacraments in general,
accomplished through interior participation.
We must learn to understand increasingly the
sacred liturgy in all its essence, to develop a living familiarity with it, so that it becomes the
soul of our daily life. It is then that we celebrate
in the correct way; it is then that the *ars cele-
brandi*, the art of celebrating, emerges by itself.
In this art there must be nothing artificial. If the
liturgy is the central duty of the priest, this also
means that prayer must be a primary reality, to
be learned ever anew and ever more deeply at
the school of Christ and of the saints of all the
ages. Since the Christian liturgy by its nature is
also always a proclamation, we must be people
who are familiar with the Word of God, love
it and live by it: only then can we explain it in
an adequate way. "To serve the Lord"—priestly
service also means precisely to learn to know the
Lord in his Word and to make it known to all
those he entrusts to us.

Lastly, two other aspects are part of service.
No one is closer to his master than the servant
who has access to the most private dimensions
of his life. In this sense "to serve" means close-
ness, it requires familiarity. This familiarity also
involves a danger: when we continually encounter the sacred, it risks becoming habitual for us.
In this way, reverential fear is extinguished.
Conditioned by all our habits, we no longer

perceive the great, new and surprising fact that he himself is present, speaks to us, gives himself to us. We must ceaselessly struggle against this becoming accustomed to the extraordinary reality, against the indifference of the heart, always recognizing our insufficiency anew and the grace that there is in the fact that he consigned himself into our hands. To serve means to draw near, but above all it also means obedience. The servant is under the word: "not my will, but thine, be done" (Lk 22:42). With this word Jesus, in the Garden of Olives, has resolved the decisive battle against sin, against the rebellion of the sinful heart. Adam's sin consisted precisely in the fact that he wanted to accomplish his own will and not God's. Humanity's temptation is always to want to be totally autonomous, to follow its own will alone and to maintain that only in this way will we be free; that only thanks to a similarly unlimited freedom would man be completely man. But this is precisely how we pit ourselves against the truth. Because the truth is that we must share our freedom with others and we can be free only in communion with them. This shared freedom can be true freedom only if we enter into what constitutes the very measure of freedom, if we enter into God's will. This fundamental obedience that is part of the human being—a person cannot be merely for and by himself—becomes still more concrete in the priest: we do not preach ourselves, but him and his Word, which we could not have invented ourselves. We proclaim the Word of Christ in the correct way only in communion with his Body. Our obedience is a believing with the Church, a thinking and speaking with the Church, serving through her. What Jesus predicted to Peter also always applies: "You will be taken where you do not want to go." This letting oneself be guided where one does not want to be led is an essential dimension of our service, and it is exactly what makes us free. In this being guided, which can be contrary to our ideas and plans, we experience something new—the wealth of God's love.

"To stand in his presence and serve him": Jesus Christ as the true High Priest of the world has conferred on these words a previously unimaginable depth. He, who as Son of God was and is the Lord, has willed to become that Servant of God which the vision of the *Book of the Prophet Isaiah* had foreseen. He has willed to be the Servant of all. He has portrayed the whole of his high priesthood in the gesture of the washing of the feet. With the gesture of love to the end he washes our dirty feet, with the humility of his service he cleanses us from the illness of our pride. Thus, he makes us able to become partakers of God's banquet. He has descended, and the true ascent of man is now accomplished in our descending with him and toward him. His elevation is the Cross. It is the deepest descent and, as love pushed to the limit, it is at the same time the culmination of the ascent, the true "elevation" of humanity. "To stand in his presence and serve him": this now means to enter into his call to serve God. The Eucharist as the presence of the descent and ascent of Christ thus always recalls, beyond itself, the many ways of service through love of neighbor. Let us ask the Lord on this day for the gift to be able to say again in this sense our "yes" to his call: "Here am I! Send me" (Is 6:8). Amen.[10]

John 17:17: the high-priestly prayer of Jesus, interpretation of priestly ordination

To conclude, I would like to reflect for another moment on several words taken from the high-priestly prayer of Jesus (Jn 17) that, on the eve of my priestly ordination, were particularly engraved on my heart. While the Synoptic Gospels report essentially the preaching of Jesus in Galilee, John—who seems to have had relations of kinship with the Temple aristocracy—relates chiefly the proclamation of Jesus in Jerusalem and mentions

[10]Benedict XVI, Homily for the Chrism Mass, Holy Thursday, March 20, 2008, in Saint Peter's Basilica in Rome, in *Insegnamenti di Benedetto XVI*, IV/1 (January-July 2008) (Città Vaticana: Libreria Editrice Vaticana, 2009), 442–46. [English translation from the Vatican website, lightly emended with reference to the Italian original.]

questions concerning the Temple and worship. In this context, Jesus' high-priestly prayer takes on a particular importance.

I do not intend to repeat here the various elements that I analyzed in volume 2 of my book on Jesus.[11] I would like to limit myself only to verses 17 and 18, which especially struck me on the eve of my priestly ordination. Here is the text: "Consecrate them" [sanctify them] in the truth; your word is truth. As you sent me into the world, so I have sent them into the world." The word "holy" [*saint*, root of sanctity] expresses God's particular nature. He alone is the Holy One. Man becomes holy insofar as he begins to be with God. To be with God is to put aside what is only me and to become one with God's whole will. Nevertheless, this liberation from myself can prove to be very painful, and it is never accomplished once and for all. However, we can also understand the term "to sanctify" to mean in a very concrete way priestly ordination, in the sense in which it implies that the living God radically claims a man in order to make him enter into his service. When the text says, "Sanctify [in some translations: consecrate] them in the truth", the Lord is asking the Father to include the Twelve in his mission, to ordain them priests.

---

[11] Ratzinger, *Jesus of Nazareth*, 2:82–102.

"Sanctify [consecrate] them in the truth." Here, it seems also that there is a discreet reference to the rite of priestly ordination in the Old Testament: the ordinand was in fact physically purified by a complete washing before putting on the sacred vestments. These two elements considered together mean that, in this way, the one sent becomes a new man. But what is a symbolic figure in the ritual of the Old Testament becomes a reality in the prayer of Jesus. The only washing that can really purify man is the truth, is Christ himself. And he is also the new garment to which the exterior cultic vestment alludes. "Sanctify [consecrate] them in the truth." This means: immerse them completely in Jesus Christ so that what Paul noted as the fundamental experience of his apostolate might prove true for them: "It is no longer I who live, but Christ who lives in me" (Gal 2:20).

Thus, on that eve of my ordination, a deep impression was left on my soul of what it means to be ordained a priest, beyond all the ceremonial aspects: it means that we must continually be purified and overcome by Christ so that he is the one who speaks and acts in us, and less and less we ourselves. It appeared to me clearly that this process, which consists of becoming one with him and renouncing what belongs only to us, lasts a whole lifetime and continually includes liberations and painful renewals.

In this sense, the words of John 17:17 pointed out to me the way that I have walked throughout my life.

Benedict XVI
Vatican City, Mater Ecclesiae Monastery
September 17, 2019

II

Loving to the End

An Ecclesiological and Pastoral
Look at Priestly Celibacy

by Robert Cardinal Sarah

"When Jesus knew that his hour had come to depart out of this world to the Father, having loved his own who were in the world, he loved them to the end" (Jn 13:1). These words of the Evangelist John solemnly introduce the great "high-priestly prayer" of Jesus after the Last Supper on Holy Thursday. They express well the dispositions of soul that are necessary for any reflection on the mystery of the priest.

How can we approach this subject without trembling? It is important to take our time and to open our souls to the breath of the Holy Spirit. The priesthood, to repeat the words of the Curé of Ars, is the love of the heart of Jesus. We must not make of it a subject of polemics, of ideological battle, or of political maneuvering. Nor can we reduce it to a question of discipline or of pastoral organization.

In these recent months, we have seen so much haste, so much excitement around the Synod on Amazonia. My bishop's heart is worried. I have met with many priests who are disoriented, disturbed, and wounded in the very depths of their spiritual life by the violent challenges to the Church's doctrine. I want to say to them again today: Be not afraid! As Benedict XVI recalled:

The priest is a gift of the Heart of Christ: a gift for the Church and for the world. From the Heart of the Son of God, brimming with love, flow all the goods of the Church. From it originates, in particular, the vocation of those men who, won over by the Lord Jesus, leave all things to devote themselves without reserve to the service of the Christian people, after the example of the Good Shepherd.[1]

Dear brother priests, I want to tell you the unvarnished truth. You seem lost, discouraged, overcome by suffering. A terrible sense of abandonment and loneliness grips your heart. In a world undermined by unbelief and indifference, an apostle inevitably suffers: a priest on fire with faith and apostolic love quickly realizes that the world in which he lives is, so to speak, upside down. Nevertheless, the mystery that dwells in you can give you the strength to live in the midst of the world. And every time the servant of "the one thing necessary" strives to put God at the heart of his life, it brings a bit of light into the darkness.

In the priesthood, the sacramental continuation of the Good Shepherd's love is at stake. Therefore I speak up so that everywhere in the Church, in

---

[1] Benedict XVI, Angelus Message of June 13, 2010. [English translation from the Vatican website (lightly emended).]

a spirit of true synodality, a calm, prayerful reflection on the spiritual reality of the sacrament of Holy Orders can commence and be renewed. And I beg those on either side: let us not go too fast! We will not be able to change things in a few months. Unless our decisions are rooted in prolonged adoration, they will have the same future as the slogans and political speeches that follow one another and fall into oblivion.

Pope Emeritus Benedict XVI has given us the gift of an extraordinary *lectio divina* in which he goes back to the biblical sources of the mystery of the priesthood. As for me, I would like very humbly to take a pastor's look at this sacrament.

Our pastoral reflection must not be enslaved to current events alone or reduced to a sociological analysis. It is urgent to nourish it through contemplation and to structure it through theology. But it must also be concrete. Indeed, I have noticed that often some are content to recall the theoretical principles without drawing from them the practical consequences. Thus, in addressing the theology of the priesthood, it is not enough to recall the value of celibacy. It is necessary also to draw the concrete ecclesiological and pastoral consequences of it.

During the Synod on Amazonia, I took the time to listen to people on the ground and to talk with experienced missionaries. These exchanges reassured me in the thought that the possibility of ordaining married men would be a pastoral catastrophe, lead to ecclesiological confusion, and obscure our understanding of the priesthood. These are the three points around which I articulate the reflection that I wish to present to you today.

A pastoral catastrophe

*The priesthood: an ontological entrance
into the "yes" of Christ the priest*

We could summarize the meditation of the pope emeritus in a few words: Jesus reveals to us in his person the fullness of the priesthood. He gives its full meaning to what was announced and roughly sketched in the Old Testament. The heart of this revelation is simple: a priest is not only a man who performs a sacrificial function. He is a man who offers himself as a sacrifice through love, following Christ. Benedict XVI thus shows us clearly and definitively that the priesthood is a "state of life": "The priest is removed from worldly bonds and given over to God, and precisely in this way, starting with God, he must be available for others, for everyone."[2] Priestly celibacy is the expression of the intention to place oneself at the disposal of the

---

[2] Benedict XVI, Homily at the Chrism Mass, Saint Peter's Basilica, Holy Thursday, April 9, 2009.

Lord and of man. Pope Benedict XVI demonstrates that priestly celibacy is not a welcome "spiritual supplement" in the priest's life. A consistent priestly life ontologically requires celibacy.

Benedict XVI, in his preceding text, shows that the transition from the priesthood of the Old Testament to the priesthood of the New Testament is revealed in the transition from a "functional sexual abstinence" to an "ontological abstinence". I think that never has a pope expressed so forcefully the necessity of priestly celibacy. We must meditate on these reflections of a man who is approaching the end of his life. At this crucial hour, one does not take speech lightly. Benedict XVI tells us also that the priesthood, because it involves offering the sacrifice of the Mass, makes a matrimonial bond impossible. I would like to underscore this last point. For a priest, the celebration of the Eucharist does not amount only to carrying out rites. The celebration of the Mass presupposes that he enters with his whole being into the great gift of Christ to the Father, into the great "yes" of Jesus to his Father: "Into your hands I commit my spirit!" (Lk 23:46). Now celibacy "is a definitive 'yes'. It is to let oneself be taken in the hand of God, to give oneself into the hands of the Lord, into his 'I'.... It is the definitive 'yes'."[3]

[3] Benedict XVI, Vigil on Saint Peter's Square, Dialogue with Priests, June 10, 2010.

If we reduce priestly celibacy to a question of discipline, of adaptation to customs and cultures, we isolate the priesthood from its foundation. In this sense, priestly celibacy is necessary for a correct understanding of the priesthood. "Part of the priesthood, moreover, is truly making oneself available to the Lord in the fullness of one's being and, consequently, finding oneself totally available to men and women. I think celibacy is a fundamental expression of this totality",[4] Benedict XVI boldly declared to the clergy of the Diocese of Bolzano, Italy.

The pastoral and missionary urgency of priestly celibacy

As a bishop, I fear that the plan to ordain married men as priests might generate a pastoral catastrophe. It would be a catastrophe for the faithful to whom they would be sent. It would be a catastrophe for the priests themselves.

How could a Christian community understand the priest if it is not obvious that he is "removed from the common sphere" and "delivered over to God"?[5] How could Christians understand

---

[4] Benedict XVI, Address to the Clergy of the Diocese of Bolzano-Bressanone, August 6, 2008, lightly emended.
[5] Ibid.

that the priest gives himself to them if he is not entirely given over to the Father? If he does not enter into Jesus' kenosis, annihilation, impoverishment? "Though he was in the form of God, [Jesus] did not count equality with God a thing to be grasped, but emptied himself, taking the form of a servant" (Phil 2:6–7). He emptied himself of what he was in an act of freedom and love. Christ's abasement even to the Cross is not simply obedient, humble conduct. It is an act of self-abandonment through love in which the Son delivers himself entirely to the Father and to humanity: this is the foundation of Christ's priesthood. How, then, could a priest keep, preserve, and claim a right to a matrimonial bond? How could he refuse to make himself a slave with Jesus the priest? This total delivering of himself in Christ is the condition for a total gift of self to everyone. He who has not given himself totally to God is not given perfectly to his brethren.

What view of the priest will some isolated, poorly evangelized populations have? Is the intention to prevent them from discovering the fullness of the Christian priesthood? In early 1976, when I was a young priest, I traveled to certain remote villages in Guinea. Some of them had not had a visit from a priest for almost ten years, because the European missionaries had been expelled in 1967 by Sékou Touré. Nevertheless, the Christians continued to teach the catechism to the children and to recite their daily prayers and the Rosary. They showed a great devotion to the Virgin Mary and gathered every Sunday to listen to the Word of God.

I had the grace of meeting these men and women who kept the faith without any sacramental support, for lack of priests. They were nourished by the Word of God and kept their faith alive through daily prayer. I will never be able to forget their unimaginable joy when I celebrated Mass, which they had not experienced for such a long time. Allow me to state forcefully and with certainty: I think that if they had ordained married men in each village, the Eucharistic hunger of the faithful would have been extinguished. The people would have been cut off from that joy of receiving another Christ in the priest. For, with the instinct of faith, poor people know that a priest who has renounced marriage gives them the gift of all his spousal love.

How many times, while walking for long hours between the villages, with a briefcase-altar on my head, under the blazing sun, I myself experienced the joy of self-giving for the Church-Bride. While traveling through swamps in a makeshift canoe, in the middle of lagoons, or while crossing dangerous torrents where we were afraid of being engulfed, I felt quite palpably the joy of being entirely dedicated to God and available, given over to his people.

How I would love it if all my confreres could someday experience the welcome of a priest in an African village that recognizes Christ the Bridegroom in him: what an explosion of joy! What festivity! The songs, the dances, the effusiveness, and the meals express the gratitude of the people for this gift of self in Christ.

The ordination of married men would deprive the young Churches that are being evangelized of this experience of the presence and of the visit of Christ, delivered and given in the person of the celibate priest. The pastoral tragedy would be immense. It would lead to an impoverishment of evangelization.

I am convinced that if a large number of Western priests or bishops are willing to relativize the greatness and the importance of celibacy, it is because they have never had the concrete experience of the gratitude of a Christian community. I am not speaking simply in human terms. I think that in this gratitude there is an experience of faith. Poor and simple people are able to discern with the eyes of faith the presence of Christ the Bridegroom of the Church in the celibate priest. This spiritual experience is fundamental in the life of a priest. It cures him forever of all forms of clericalism. Having experienced it in the flesh,

I know that Christians see in me Christ who is delivered for them, and not my limited person with its qualities and its many defects.

Without this concrete experience, celibacy becomes a burden too heavy to carry. I get the impression that for some bishops from the West or even from South America, celibacy has become a heavy load. They remain faithful to it but no longer feel that they have the courage to impose it on future priests and on Christian communities because they themselves suffer from it. I understand them. Who could impose a burden on others without loving its deep meaning? Would that not be pharisaical?

Nevertheless, I am certain that there is an error of perspective here. Although it is sometimes a trial, priestly celibacy, correctly understood, is liberating. It allows the priest to become established quite consistently in his identity as spouse of the Church.

A plan that consisted of depriving communities and priests of this joy would not be a work of mercy. As a son of Africa, I cannot in conscience support the idea that people who are being evangelized should be deprived of this encounter with a priesthood that is fully lived out. The peoples of Amazonia have the right to a full experience of Christ the Bridegroom. We cannot offer them "second-class" priests.

On the contrary, the younger a Church is, the more she needs an encounter with the radical character of the Gospel. When Saint Paul exhorts the young Christian communities of Ephesus, Philippi, and Colossae, he does not confront them with an unattainable ideal but, rather, teaches them all the demands of the Gospel: "As therefore you received Christ Jesus the Lord, so live in him, rooted and built up in him and established in the faith, just as you were taught, abounding in thanksgiving. See to it that no one makes a prey of you [*in French:* reduces you to slavery] by philosophy and empty deceit, according to human tradition, according to the elemental spirits of the universe, and not according to Christ" (Col 2:6–8). In this teaching there is neither rigidity nor intolerance. The Word of God demands a radical conversion. It is incompatible with compromises and ambiguities. It is "living and active, sharper than any two-edged sword" (Heb 4:12). Following Paul's example, we must preach with clarity and gentleness, without polemical harshness or half-hearted timidity.

Allow me to refer once again to my personal experience. In my childhood, I lived in a world that had barely emerged from paganism. My parents did not know Christianity until they were adults. My father was baptized two years after my birth. My grandmother received

Baptism at the moment of her death. Therefore, I was well acquainted with animism and the traditional religion. I know the difficulty of evangelization, the painful uprooting and the heroic changes that neophytes must confront with regard to pagan customs, ways of life, and traditions. I imagine what the evangelization of my village would have been like if a married man had been ordained a priest there. The thought of it wrenches my heart. What sadness! I certainly would not be a priest today, because the radical character of the missionaries' life is what attracted me.

How dare we deprive peoples of the joy of such an encounter with Christ? I consider that a contemptuous attitude. Some have exploited and hardened the opposition between "pastoral care by visit" and "pastoral care of presence". The visit to a community by a missionary priest who has come from a distant land expresses the solicitude of the Universal Church. It is the image of the Word visiting humanity. The ordination of a married man in the midst of the community would express the opposite movement: as if each community were bound to find the means of salvation within itself.

When the great missionary Saint Paul tells us about his visits to the communities in Asia Minor that he himself founded, he gives us the example of an apostle visiting the Christian communities in order to strengthen them.

God's mercy becomes incarnate in Christ's visit. We receive it with gratitude. For us it is an opening onto the whole ecclesial family. I fear that the ordination of married men who are responsible for a community might close that community in on itself and cut it off from the universality of the Church. How could anyone ask a married man to change his community, while taking his wife and children along with him? How could he experience the freedom of a servant who is ready to give himself to everyone?

The priesthood is a gift that is received as the Incarnation of the Word is received. It is neither a right nor an obligation. A community that was formed according to the idea of a "right to the Eucharist" would no longer be a disciple of Christ. As its name indicates, the Eucharist is thanksgiving, a gratuitous gift, a merciful present. The Eucharistic presence is received with wonder and joy as an unmerited gift. Any believer who claims it as his due shows that he is incapable of understanding it.

I am persuaded that the Christian communities of Amazonia themselves do not think along the lines of Eucharistic demands. I think, rather, that these topics are obsessions that stem from theological milieus at universities. We are dealing with ideologies developed by a few theologians, or rather sorcerer's apprentices, who wish to utilize the distress of poor peoples as an experimental laboratory for their clever plans. I cannot resolve to be silent and let them do so. I want to take up the defense of the poor, the little ones, these people who have "no voice". Let us not deprive them of the fullness of the priesthood. Let us not deprive them of the true meaning of the Eucharist. We cannot "tamper with [*trafiquer*] the Catholic doctrine of the priesthood and celibacy in order to tailor-make a response to the felt or alleged needs of some extreme pastoral situations", Marc Cardinal Ouellet recently remarked. "Above all, I think that the Latin Church does not know her own tradition of celibacy, which goes back to apostolic times and was the secret and the driving force of her strong missionary expansion."[6] The point we are talking about is of capital importance. Priestly celibacy is a powerful driving force of evangelization. It makes the missionary credible. More radically, it makes him free, ready to go anywhere and to risk everything because he is no longer detained by any place.

In light of Church tradition

Some will think that my reflection is mistaken. Some will tell me that priestly celibacy is only a

---

[6] Marc Cardinal Ouellet, Interview with Jean-Marie Guénois, *Le Figaro*, October 28, 2019.

discipline that was imposed at a late date by the Latin Church on her clerics.

I have read such statements, which are repeated in many newspapers. Historical honesty obliges me to declare that they are false. Serious historians know that from the fourth century on, the councils recall the necessity of continence for priests.[7] We must be precise. Many married men were ordained priests during the first millennium. But from the day of their ordination on, they were obliged to abstain from sexual relations with their wives. This point is regularly recalled by the councils, which rely on a tradition received from the apostles. Is it conceivable that the Church could have brutally introduced this discipline of clerical continence without causing a general outcry among those on whom it would be imposed? Now historians emphasize the absence of protests when the Council of Elvira, at the very beginning of the fourth century, decided to exclude from the clerical state those bishops, priests, and deacons who were suspected of engaging in sexual relations with

[7] On this subject, one can read the historical study by Christian Cochini, *The Apostolic Origins of Priestly Celibacy*, trans. Nelly Marans (San Francisco: Ignatius Press, 1990); see also: Alfons Maria Cardinal Stickler, *The Case for Clerical Celibacy: Its Historical Development and Theological Foundations*, trans. Fr. Brian Ferme (San Francisco: Ignatius Press, 1995); or Stefan Heid, *Celibacy in the Early Church: The Beginnings of a Discipline of Obligatory Continence for Clerics in East and West*, trans. Michael J. Miller (San Francisco: Ignatius Press, 2000; original German ed., 1997).

their wives. The fact that such a demanding decision aroused no opposition proves that the law of
clerical continence was not something new. The
Church had just emerged from the period of per-
secutions. One of her first concerns was to recall
a rule that may occasionally have been bent in
the turmoil of the age of martyrs but was already
well established.

Some commentators show terrible intellectual dishonesty. They tell us: there were married
priests. That is true. But they were obliged to
practice complete continence. Do we want to go
back to that state of affairs? The esteem in which
we hold the sacrament of Matrimony and the
better understanding that we have of it since the
council forbid it.

The priesthood is a response to a personal vocation. It is the fruit of an intimate call from God,
the archetype of which is God's call to Samuel (1
Sam 3). A man does not become a priest because
it is necessary to fill a need of the community and
someone has to occupy the "position". Priesthood is a state of life. It is the fruit of an intimate
dialogue between God who calls and the soul
that responds: "Behold, I have come to do your
will" (Heb 10:7). Nothing can interfere with this
heart-to-heart conversation. Only the Church can
authenticate the response to it. I wonder: What
will happen to the wife of a man who has been
ordained a priest? What place will there be for

her? Is there a vocation to be the wife of a priest? The priesthood, as we have seen, presupposes handing over one's whole life, delivering oneself up as Christ did. It presupposes an absolute gift of self to God and a total gift of self to the brethren. What place can be reserved, then, for the conjugal bond? Vatican Council II brought out the dignity of the sacrament of Matrimony as the proper path to sanctity through conjugal life. This state of life presupposes, however, that the spouses place the bond that unites them above all else. To ordain a married man a priest would amount to diminishing the dignity of marriage and reducing the priesthood to a job [*fonction*].

What is to be said about the freedom to which the couple's children can legitimately aspire? Must they, too, embrace their father's vocation? How can anyone impose on them a way of life that they did not choose? They have the right to enjoy all the resources necessary for their flourishing. Will married priests have to be paid accordingly as a consequence?

One could argue that the Christian East has always been familiar with this situation and that it poses no problem. That is false. At a late date, the Christian East allowed married men who had become priests to have sexual relations with their spouses. This discipline was introduced at the Council in Trullo in 691. The novelty appeared as a result of an error in transcribing the canons of the council that had been held in 390 in Carthage. The major innovation of this seventh-century council, moreover, is not the disappearance of priestly continence but the limitation of it to the periods preceding the celebration of the Holy Mysteries. The ontological bond between priestly ministry and continence is still established and perceived. Does anyone want to go back to that practice? We must listen to the testimonies coming from the Eastern Catholic Churches. Several members of these Churches have clearly emphasized that the priestly state came into tension with the married state. Over the past centuries, it has been possible for the situation to persist thanks to the existence of "families of priests" in which the children were educated to "take part" in the vocation of the father of the family and in which the daughters often married a future priest. A better appreciation of the dignity and of the freedom of each person makes this *modus operandi* impossible now.[8] The Eastern married clergy is in crisis. Divorce by priests has become a cause of ecumenical tension among the Orthodox Patriarchates.

---

[8] Several years ago, the president of an Orthodox association of priests observed that the percentage of married clerics was constantly decreasing in Greece (three thousand out of eleven thousand men in all). He identified the cause of it: fewer and fewer emancipated women agree to lead the demanding life of a cleric's wife. (See https://www .temesdavui.org/node/6549.)

In the separated Eastern Churches, only the preponderant presence of monks makes association with a married clergy acceptable to the people of God. There are many Orthodox Christians who would never go to confession to a married priest. The *sensus fidei* causes the faithful to discern a form of incompleteness in the clergy who do not live out consecrated celibacy.

Why does the Catholic Church allow the presence of a married clergy in some Eastern Churches in union with Rome? In light of the statements of the recent Magisterium on the ontological bond between priesthood and celibacy, I think that the purpose of this acceptance is to foster a gradual development toward the practice of celibacy, which would take place, not by a disciplinarian path, but rather for properly spiritual and pastoral reasons.[9]

Ecclesiological confusion

In light of Vatican Council II

In his opening address to the second session of the council, Pope Saint Paul VI had asked the

---

[9] See F. Frost, "Le célibat sacerdotal, signe d'espérance pour tout le christianisme", in *Le Célibat sacerdotal, fondements, joies, défis*, Actes du colloque d'Ars (Paris: Parole et Silence, 2011), 180–81.

Council Fathers to start reflecting theologically on the three states of life that constitute the ecclesial communion: the priestly state of life, the conjugal state of life, and the religious state of life. Paul VI intended thus to promote "a deeper awareness by the Church of what she is". This program was implemented by Pope John Paul II during three postconciliar synods dedicated to these states of life.

The synod on the subject of the priesthood made it possible to compose in 1992 the Apostolic Exhortation *Pastores Dabo Vobis*. In it, Saint John Paul II forcefully teaches that priestly celibacy follows from what the council described as the essence of the character and of the grace proper to the sacrament of Holy Orders: the enablement to represent Christ the Head for the Body that is the Church-Bride. The Church, as the Bride of Jesus Christ, desires to be loved by the priest in the total, exclusive manner in which Jesus Christ the Head and Bridegroom loved her.[10] This statement by Saint John Paul II is of capital importance. It holds up celibacy as a need of the Church. The Church needs men who love with the very love of Christ the Bridegroom.

Without the presence of the celibate priest, the Church can no longer become aware that she

---

[10] John Paul II, Apostolic Exhortation *Pastores Dabo Vobis*, March 15, 1992, no. 29.

is the Bride of Christ. Priestly celibacy, far from being merely an ascetical discipline, is necessary to the identity of the Church. You can say that the Church would no longer understand herself if she were no longer loved totally by celibate priests who sacramentally represent Christ the Bridegroom.

Sacrament of Holy Orders and sacrament of Matrimony

This renewed understanding of celibacy is the fruit of Vatican Council II, which made it possible to rediscover the patristic theme of the divine plan. From the origin, the Creator's intention is to enter into a nuptial dialogue with his creation. This vocation is inscribed on the heart of man and of woman. Through the sacrament of Matrimony, the mutual love of the spouses in all its corporeal, psychological, and spiritual dimensions is integrated into Christ's love for humanity.

In loving each other, the spouses participate in the mystery of Christ's love. They enter into this wedding, of which the nuptial bed is the Cross. "Husbands, love your wives, as Christ loved the Church and gave himself up for her.... 'For this reason a man shall leave his father and mother and be joined to his wife, and the two shall become one flesh.' This is a great mystery, and I mean in reference to Christ and the Church" (Eph

5:25, 31–32). This spousal vocation, inscribed on the heart of every person, includes an appeal to the total and exclusive gift of self, following the example of the gift of the Cross. Celibacy is for the priest the means of entering into an authentic vocation as spouse.[11] His gift to the Church is taken up and integrated into the gift of Christ the Bridegroom to the Church his Bride.[12] There is a true analogy between the sacrament of Matrimony and the sacrament of Holy Orders, both of which culminate in a total gift of self. This is why the two sacraments are mutually exclusive.

> Christ's gift of himself ... is described in terms of that unique gift of self made by the bridegroom to the bride.... Jesus is the true Bridegroom who offers to the Church the wine of salvation (cf. Jn 2:11).... The Church ... is also the bride who proceeds like a new Eve from the open side of the redeemer on the cross. Hence Christ stands "before" the Church and "nourishes and cherishes her" (cf. Eph 5:29), giving his life for

---

[11] "In virginity and celibacy, chastity retains its original meaning, that is, of human sexuality lived as a genuine sign of and precious service to the love of communion and gift of self to others. This meaning is fully found in virginity which makes evident, even in the renunciation of marriage, the 'nuptial meaning' of the body through a communion and a personal gift to Jesus Christ and his Church" (ibid.).

[12] On this subject, the reader may consult the very inspiring study by Frédéric Dumas, *Prêtre et époux? Lettre ouverte à mon frère prêtre* [Priest and spouse? Open letter to my brother priest] (Paris: Mame, 2018).

her. The priest is called to be the living image of Jesus Christ, the spouse of the Church.... In virtue of his configuration to Christ, the head and shepherd, the priest stands in this spousal relationship with regard to the community.[13]

The priest's capacity for spousal love is entirely given to and reserved for the Church. The logic of the priesthood excludes any "other spouse" than the Church. The priest's capacity for love must be taken up completely [*épuisée*] by the Church.[14] Saint John Paul II goes on to write:

In his spiritual life, therefore, he is called to live out Christ's spousal love toward the Church, his bride. Therefore, the priest's life ought to radiate this spousal character, which demands that he be a witness to Christ's spousal love and thus be capable of loving people with a heart which is new, generous and pure—with genuine self-detachment, with full, constant and faithful dedication and at the same time with a kind of "divine jealousy" (cf. 2 Cor 11:2) and even with a kind of maternal tenderness, capable of bearing

[13] John Paul II, *Pastores Dabo Vobis*, no. 22.

[14] Marianne Schlosser, in her beautiful intervention at the Symposium on "Contemporary Challenges for Holy Orders", organized by the Ratzinger *Schülerkreise* [circle of former students] in Rome on September 28, 2019, quoted an eighth-century Syrian author: "The priest is the father of all the faithful, both of the men and of the women. And so, if he is in this situation with regard to the faithful and he marries, he can be compared to a man who marries his own daughter."

"the pangs of birth" until "Christ be formed" in the faithful (cf. Gal 4:19).[15]

A Church that had no experience of being loved by celibate priests would end up no longer grasping the nuptial meaning of all sanctity. Indeed, priestly celibacy and marriage go hand in hand. If the one is called into question, the other fails. Priests point out to spouses the meaning of the total gift. Spouses, by their conjugal life, point out to priests the meaning of their celibacy. To call celibacy into question affects the meaning of marriage, too. Benedict XVI had had a premonition of this. He returned to the subject several times: "Celibacy ... is a definitive 'yes'.... It is an act of loyalty and trust, an act that also implies the fidelity of marriage.... It is the definitive 'yes' that supposes, confirms the definitive 'yes' of marriage."[16] Interfering with priestly celibacy is tantamount to injuring the Christian meaning of marriage. In order understand this mystery, Cardinal Ratzinger continues,

> The candidate for the priesthood has to recognize the faith as a force in his life, and he must know that he can live celibacy only in faith. Then celibacy can also become again a testimony that says something to people and that also gives

[15]John Paul II, *Pastores Dabo Vobis*, no. 22.
[16]Benedict XVI, Vigil on Saint Peter's Square, Dialogue with Priests, June 10, 2010.

them the courage to marry. The two institutions are interconnected. If fidelity in the one is no longer possible, the other no longer exists: one fidelity sustains the other.... Basically, then, the question is posed thus: Does the possibility of a definitive choice belong in the central sphere of man's existence as an essential component? In deciding his form of life, can he commit himself to a definitive bond? I would say two things. He can do so only if he is really anchored in his faith. Second, only then does he also reach the full form of human love and human maturity.[17]

In countries that are just being evangelized, the discovery of the vocation of spouses to holiness is often a challenge. Sometimes the meaning of marriage is distorted; the dignity of the woman is trampled on. I think that there is a serious problem here. In order to remedy it, we must teach everyone the necessity of living out marriage as a total gift of self. But how can a priest be credible to spouses unless he himself lives out his priesthood as an absolute gift of self?

The Sacrament of Holy Orders and the place of the woman

The weakening of celibacy shakes the ecclesial edifice as a whole. In fact, debates about celibacy

[17]Joseph Ratzinger, *Salt of the Earth*, trans. Adrian Walker (San Francisco: Ignatius Press, 1997), 197.

naturally give rise to questions about the possibility of women being ordained as priests or
deacons. This question, nevertheless, was settled
definitively by Saint John Paul II in the Apostolic
Letter *Ordinatio Sacerdotalis* dated May 22, 1994,
in which he proclaims "that the Church has no
authority whatsoever to confer priestly ordination
on women, and that this judgment is to be definitively held by all the Church's faithful". To dis-
pute this reveals an ignorance of the true nature
of the Church.

Indeed, the economy of salvation integrates the
Creator's plan of complementarity between man
and woman into the spousal relation between
Jesus and his Bride the Church. Through his
representation of Christ the Bridegroom, into
which the fact that he is of the male sex is completely integrated, the priest thus finds himself in
a relation of complementarity with woman, who
represents in an iconic way the Bride-Church.
Promoting the ordination of women amounts to
denying their identity and the place of each sex.

We need women's special genius. We must
learn from them what the Church must be. For
in the heart of every woman, as John Paul II
declared, there is a fundamental disposition to
receive love.[18] Now the Church is essentially the

---

[18] Cf. John Paul II, Apostolic Letter *Mulieris Dignitatem*, August 15,
1965, no. 29.

receiving of Jesus' virginal love. She is a response through faith to the Bridegroom's love. I dare say that the Church is fundamentally feminine; she cannot do without women.

> In the Church, woman as "sign" is more than ever central and fruitful, following as it does from the very identity of the Church, as received from God and accepted in faith. It is this "mystical" identity, profound and essential, which needs to be kept in mind when reflecting on the respective roles of men and women in the Church....
>
> Far from giving the Church an identity based on an historically conditioned model of femininity, the reference to Mary, with her dispositions of listening, welcoming, humility, faithfulness, praise and waiting, places the Church in continuity with the spiritual history of Israel.... While these traits should be characteristic of every baptized person, women in fact live them with particular intensity and naturalness. In this way, women play a role of maximum importance in the Church's life by recalling these dispositions to all the baptized and contributing in a unique way to showing the true face of the Church, spouse of Christ and mother of believers....
>
> Women are called to be unique examples and witnesses for all Christians of how the Bride is to respond in love to the love of the Bridegroom.[19]

[19] Congregation for the Doctrine of the Faith, *Letter to the Bishops of the Catholic Church on the Collaboration of Men and Women in the Church and in the World*, July 31, 2004, nos. 15–16.

The government of the Church is a loving service of the bridegroom for the bride. Therefore it can be carried out only by men who are identified with Christ, the Bridegroom and Servant, through the sacramental character of priesthood. If we make it the object of rivalry between men and women, we reduce it to a form of political, worldly power. Then it loses its specific nature, which is to be a way of participating in Christ's action.

Nowadays cleverly orchestrated media campaigns are calling for the female diaconate. What are they looking for? What is hidden behind these strange political demands?

The worldly mind-set of "equality" is at work. They are stirring up a sort of mutual jealousy between men and women that can only be sterile.

I think that we must study in greater depth the place of the feminine charism. Formerly, speech was freer than it is today, and women's speech in particular had a central place. Their role was firmly to remind the whole institution about the necessity of sanctity. It is good to recollect, by way of example, the admonition sent by Catherine of Siena to Gregory XI, in which she reminds him of his identification with Christ, the Bridegroom of the Church: "Because your burden is greater you need a more bold, courageous heart, fearful of nothing that might happen. For you know well, Most Holy Father, that when you accepted Holy Church as your bride you agreed also to work hard for her."[20] What bishop, what pope would let himself be challenged today so vehemently? Today, voices eager for polemics would immediately describe Catherine of Siena as an enemy of the pope or as a leader of his opponents. Former centuries had much greater liberty than ours: they witnessed women holding a charismatic place. Their role was firmly to remind the whole institution about the necessity of sanctity.

> Thus, the Church has a great debt of gratitude to women.... At a charismatic level, women do so much, I would dare to say, for the government of the Church, starting with women Religious, with the Sisters of the great Fathers of the Church ... to the great women of the Middle Ages—Saint Hildegard, Saint Catherine of Siena, then Saint Teresa of Avila—and lastly, Mother Teresa of Calcutta. I would say that this charismatic sector is undoubtedly distinct from the ministerial sector in the strict sense of the term, but it is a true and deep participation in the government of the Church.

[20] Saint Catherine of Siena, Letter 252, *To Pope Gregory XI*, in *The Letters of Catherine of Siena*, vol. 2, trans. Suzanne Noffke, O.P. (Tempe, Ariz.: Arizona Center for Medieval and Renaissance Studies, 2001), 269–73 at 271, lightly emended.

How could we imagine the government of the Church without this contribution, which sometimes becomes very visible, such as when Saint Hildegard criticized the bishops or when Saint Bridget offered recommendations and Saint Catherine of Siena obtained the return of the Popes to Rome? It has always been a crucial factor without which the Church cannot survive.[21]

Appreciation for the specific qualities of women is not achieved by way of female "ministries" that would only be arbitrary, artificial creations with no future. We know, for example, that the women who were called "deaconesses" were not recipients of the sacrament of Holy Orders. Ancient sources are unanimous in forbidding deaconesses to have any ministry at the altar during the liturgy. Their sole liturgical function in the region of Syria would have been to perform the pre-baptismal anointing of the entire body of women. Indeed, before the Baptism properly speaking, immediately after the renunciation of Satan, the neophyte was anointed with exorcised oil, which we now call the "oil of catechumens". We can suppose that they anointed at least the breast and the shoulders. In the case of women, this therefore posed

---

[21]Benedict XVI, Address to the Clergy of Rome, March 2, 2006, lightly emended.

a delicate problem of modesty. And so, in some localities, deaconesses would have been put in charge of this part of the ceremony.[22]

It is enlightening to dwell on what history and the past have bequeathed to us. Saint John Henry Cardinal Newman underscored this eloquently: "The history of the past ends in the present; and the present is our scene of trial; and to behave ourselves towards its various phenomena duly and religiously, we must understand them; and to understand them, we must have recourse to those past events which led to them. Thus the present is a text, and the past its interpretation."[23] Now the fact is clearly established that the deaconesses were not ordained, but only blessed, as the Chaldean

---

[22] See Aimé Georges Martimort, *Deaconesses: An Historical Study* (San Francisco: Ignatius Press, 1986), 58 and passim. The oldest mention of their function is found in the *Teachings of the Apostles*, which dates back to the third century and probably reflect the customs of Syria and the Trans-Jordan. In this collection, the bishop is advised to designate a woman to serve the female catechumens: "When women go down to the water, it is necessary that they be anointed by a deaconess ... [with] the anointing oil.... When there is a woman, and especially a deaconess, it is not fitting for the women that they be seen by the men, but that by the laying on of the hand the head alone be anointed.... Let a man repeat over them the names of the invocation of the Godhead" (*Didascalia Apostolorum*, 16; translated from the Syriac by Margaret Dunlop Gibson [London: C.J. Clay and Sons, 1903], 78).

[23] John Henry Newman, "Reformation of the Eleventh Century", in *Essays Critical and Historical*, vol. 2 (London and New York: Longmans, Green and Co., 1914), 250.

Pontifical specifies explicitly.[24] Nothing in tradition justifies the proposal today to ordain "deaconesses". This desire is the product of a mentality resulting from a false feminism that denies the profound identity of women. This temptation, which aims to clericalize women, is the final metamorphosis of clericalism, the resurgence of which Pope Francis has rightly denounced. Would women not be respectable unless they were clerics? In the Church, is the clerical state the only way to exist and to have a place? We must give women their entire place as women and not just grant them a little bit of the men's place! That would be a tragic illusion. Indeed, it would be tantamount to forgetting the necessary ecclesial balance between charism and institution.

Questioning priestly celibacy is decidedly a source of confusion about the role of everyone in the Church: men, women, spouses, the priest.

---

[24] See J. M. Vosté, *Pontificale Syrorum orientalium, id est Chaldeorum, Versio latina* (Vatican City: Typis polyglottis Vaticanis, 1937–1938), 82–83. We find very clear specifications in the *Canonical Resolutions* of James of Edessa in the seventh century: "The deaconess has no power at the altar, because when she is instituted, this is not done in the name of the altar, but she stands in the church. This is her only power: to sweep the sanctuary and to light the sanctuary lamp, and she may do these two things only if there is no deacon or priest nearby.... She must not touch the altar. She anoints the adult women when they are baptized; she visits and cares for sick women. That is the only power of the deaconesses" (*Synodicon syrien*, ed. A. Voöbus, CSCO 368, p. 242).

Sacrament of Holy Orders and Baptism

The recent debates of the Synod on Amazonia brought to light a new confusion about the meaning of Baptism and Confirmation.

I was anxious to be present during all the debates in the synod hall. I listened to speaker after speaker emphasize the need to make a transition from pastoral care by visitation to pastoral care of presence and consequently demand the ordination of married permanent deacons to the priesthood. It was emphasized that the communities of Evangelical Protestants have managed to implement this pastoral care of presence—even though, as we emphasized above, their ecclesial communities reject the priesthood.

The Amazonian Christian communities have an urgent need of a "*diakonia* [service] of faith". When I heard these words pronounced by a Synod Father, I recalled my years as a young bishop in a diocese in which the priests were few in number. I had determined then that the essential element of my missionary work would have to be to strengthen the formation of catechists. They were the true builders of our parishes. I remember the great gratitude that I felt in seeing them walk for long hours to go from village to village and work selflessly to hand on the faith. I think that commentators now neglect all the dynamic potentialities contained in the sacraments of Baptism and Confirmation. A baptized and confirmed Christian must become, as Pope Francis puts it, a "missionary disciple". It is up to the baptized first to be responsible for this presence of the faith. Why would anyone want to clericalize them at all costs? Have they no faith in the grace of Confirmation that makes us witnesses to Christ? Should we reserve to clerics alone the task of proclaiming Jesus and witnessing to him? Here again, we are heading toward an ecclesiological confusion. Vatican II invited us to acknowledge the role of the laity in the Church's mission: "The laity derive the right and duty to the apostolate from their union with Christ the head; incorporated into Christ's Mystical Body through Baptism and strengthened by the power of the Holy Spirit through Confirmation, they are assigned to the apostolate by the Lord Himself."[25]

If we limit the presence of the Church to a clerical presence, we lose the essential contribution of the conciliar ecclesiology. Wherever a baptized person is present, the Church is alive. Wherever a confirmed person spreads the Gospel, Christ proclaims it in him. Will we have the

---

[25] Vatican II, Decree on the Apostolate of the Laity *Apostolicam Actuositatem*, November 18, 1965, no. 3.

courage to emerge from our clerical mentality? The history of the missions invites us to do so. I would like to take the time to go back to it.

The Church in Japan, founded by Saint Francis Xavier in 1549, was very quickly persecuted. The missionaries were martyred and expelled. The Christians lived for two centuries without a priestly presence. Nevertheless, they continued to hand on the faith and Baptism. In these Christian communities, the baptized had divided up the services of head of the community and of catechist. Baptism had given to them all its fruits of dynamism and apostolate.

Each generation of the Christians in Japan taught the three signs by which they would recognize the return of the priests among them: "They will be celibate, they will have a statue of Mary, they will obey the Pope of Rome."[26] Intuitively, the believers had identified priestly celibacy as a "mark" revealing the nature of the priesthood and of the Church.

In Korea, to take another example, the Church was born of evangelization by baptized laymen, including Paul Chong Hasang and Francis Choi Kyung-Hwan. In Uganda, the martyrs Charles

[26] See Shinzo Kawamura, S.J., *Pope Pius IX and Japan: The History of an Oriental Miracle*, Pontifical Gregorian University, Symposium on the 75th Anniversary of Diplomatic Relations between Japan and the Holy See (Rome, 2017).

Lwanga, Andrew Kaggwa, Denis Ssebuggwawo, Pontian Ngondwe, John Kizito, and their companions were all young Christians who had grown up without a priest yet were strongly attached to Christ, to the point of agreeing to give up their lives for him.

I would like to cite also the very beautiful testimony of a priest who was present at the Synod on Amazonia, a priest who had been a missionary for twenty-five years in Angola: "Once the civil war ended in 2002, I was able to visit Christian communities that, for thirty years, had not had the Eucharist, nor seen a priest, but remained firm in the faith and were dynamic communities, led by the 'catechist', which is a fundamental ministry in Africa, and by other ministers: evangelizers, prayer leaders, the pastoral care of women, service to the poorest."[27]

These different examples emphasize that priestly celibacy and baptismal dynamism reinforce each other. The ordination of married men would give an unfortunate signal that the laity is being clericalized. It would result in a weakening of the missionary zeal of the lay faithful by causing them to think that mission work was reserved for clerics.

[27] Martin Lasarte, "Amazon Synod: Are Married Priests Really a Solution?" (Part One), *AsiaNews.it*, October 10, 2019. This testimony was published on the website of the Pontifical Institute for Foreign Missions (PIME).

From the ecclesiological perspective, therefore, the ordination of married men would produce a true confusion about the states of life. It would obscure the meaning of marriage and would weaken the apostolate of the baptized. It would prevent the Church from understanding herself as the dearly beloved Bride of Christ and would result in confusion about the true place of women within the Church.

I do not dare to imagine the very serious harm that it would cause to the unity of the Universal Church if it was left up to each episcopal conference to make such an option available in its territory.

A major ecclesiological issue

These confusions reveal a deep-seated ecclesiological error. Today the temptation is for us to reason in a purely pragmatic [*fonctionnelle*] way. Indeed, the shortage of priests in some regions is real. Even so, is it necessary to respond to it by taking human effectiveness as the sole criterion? Do we regard the Church as a sociological institution or as the Mystical Body of Christ, enlivened by charisms, the gratuitous gifts offered by the Holy Spirit?

In a profound reflection, Cardinal Ratzinger wondered:

For what are the fundamental institutional elements in the Church, which constantly bring
order in her life and make their mark on her?
Certainly, sacramental office in its various
grades—the office of bishop, priest, and deacon: the sacrament that most significantly goes
by the name of *ordo* is the ultimate and only
enduring and obligatory structure that constitutes, so to speak, the predetermined set form
of organization in the Church and that makes
her an "institution". Yet only in our own century has it become customary—perhaps for the
practical purposes of ecumenism—to refer to
the sacrament of *ordo* as "ministry", whereby
it then appears entirely in the light of an institution, as being institutional. Yet this "office" is a
"sacrament", and thereby we quite clearly pass
beyond the normal sociological understanding of
institutions. The fact that this, the sole enduring
structural element in the Church, is a sacrament
means at the same time that it is always having to
be constituted anew by God. The Church cannot dispose of it as she wishes; it is not just there
and cannot be set up or arranged by the Church
out of her own resources. It comes into being
only secondarily through the Church's call; pri-
marily it is through God's call to this particular
person and, thus, only charismatically and pneu-
matologically. It can therefore be accepted and
lived out only on the basis of the way the calling is renewed, of the way the Spirit cannot be

predicted or controlled. Because that is how it is, because the Church cannot simply of herself appoint "officials" but has to wait on God's call— and this is ultimately the only reason—there can be a shortage of priests. Hence it has always been the case that this office cannot simply be created by the institution but has to be asked of God in prayer. Jesus' saying has always been true: "The harvest is plentiful, but the laborers are few; pray therefore the Lord of the harvest to send out laborers into his harvest" (Mt 9:37f.). On that basis we can also understand how the calling of the Twelve was the fruit of a night in prayer by Jesus (Lk 6:12ff.).

The Latin Church has explicitly emphasized the strictly charismatic character of the priestly ministry by linking priesthood (following in this a very old tradition in the Church) with celibacy, which quite clearly can be understood only as a personal charism, never simply as a quality of the office. The demand for separating priesthood and celibacy ultimately rests on the idea that priesthood ought to be regarded, not as charismatic, but—for the sake of the institution and its needs—purely as an office that can be assigned by the institution itself. If you want to take priesthood so entirely under your own management, with its accompanying institutional security, then the link with the charismatic aspect found in the demand for celibacy is a scandal to be removed as quickly as possible. In that case, however, the Church as a whole is being understood as a merely human organization, and the security you are aiming for does not bring the results it is supposed to achieve. From the fact that the Church is not our institution but is the breakthrough of something different, that she is in her nature *iuris divini* [of divine right], it follows that we cannot ever simply constitute her ourselves. That means that we can never apply to her purely institutional criteria; it means that she is entirely herself at the very point at which the standards and methods of human institutions are broken through.[28]

This shows the magnitude of any modification of the law of celibacy. It is the touchstone of any sound ecclesiology. Celibacy is a rampart that enables the Church to avoid the trap that would amount to understanding her as a human institution whose laws would be effectiveness and functionality. Priestly celibacy opens the door to gratuitousness in the ecclesial body. It protects the initiative of the Holy Spirit and prevents us from thinking that we are the masters and creators of the Church. We must take seriously the

---

[28] Joseph Ratzinger, "Church Movements and Their Place in Theology", in *Pilgrim Fellowship of Faith: The Church as Communion*, trans. Henry Taylor (San Francisco: Ignatius Press, 2005), 176–208 at 178–80, lightly emended.

statement by Saint John Paul II: "Priestly celibacy should not be considered just as a legal norm or as a totally external condition for admission to ordination, but rather as a value that is profoundly connected with ordination, whereby a man takes on the likeness of Jesus Christ, the good shepherd and spouse of the Church."[29] Celibacy expresses and manifests how much the Church is the work of the Good Shepherd before it is ours. However, as Joseph Ratzinger again noted:

> In the Church, besides this really basic order—the sacrament—there are of course also institutions of purely human law for the many purposes of management, organization, and coordination, which may grow in accordance with the demands of the time and may have to grow. Yet we would have to say this: the Church needs such institutions of her own, yet if they become too numerous and too strong, then they threaten the order and the life of her spiritual essence.[30]

The proposal to create "ministries" is part of this institutional framework "of human right", which can be somewhat useful but is not of primary importance. It is sometimes necessary for the sake of the mission to go ahead with such creations.

[29] John Paul II, *Pastores Dabo Vobis*, no. 50.
[30] Ratzinger, "Church Movements", in *Pilgrim Fellowship*, 180–81.

On this subject, the Instruction *Ecclesia de Mysterio*, published on August 15, 1997, under the title *On Certain Questions regarding the Collaboration of the Non-Ordained Faithful in the Sacred Ministry of Priest*, approved by Pope John Paul II and signed by eight heads of dicasteries, remains the definitive authority that must guide our actions. It elaborates and completes the Motu Proprio *Ministeria Quaedam* published in 1972 by Paul VI to suppress the minor orders. The document recalls that the use of the word "ministry" is not without ambiguity:

> For some time now, it has been customary to use the word *ministries* not only for the *officia* (*offices*) and non-ordained *munera* (*functions*) exercised by Pastors in virtue of the sacrament of Orders, but also for those exercised by the lay faithful in virtue of their baptismal priesthood. The terminological question becomes even more complex and delicate when all the faithful are recognized as having the possibility of supplying—by official deputation given by the Pastors—certain functions more proper to clerics, which, nevertheless, do not require the character of Orders. It must be admitted that the language becomes doubtful, confused, and hence not helpful for expressing the doctrine of the faith whenever the difference "of essence and not merely of degree" between the baptismal

priesthood and the ordained priesthood is in any way obscured.[31]

Consequently, it is advisable to recall that

[t]he *officia* temporarily entrusted to [the lay faithful], however, are exclusively the result of a deputation by the Church. Only with constant reference to the one source, the 'ministry of Christ' (...) may the term *ministry* be applied to a certain extent and without ambiguity to the lay faithful: that is, without it being perceived and lived as an undue aspiration to the *ordained ministry* or as a progressive erosion of its specific nature.

In this original sense the term *ministry (servitium)* expresses only the work by which the Church's members continue the mission and ministry of Christ within her and the whole world. However, when the term is distinguished from and compared with the various *munera* and *officia*, then it should be clearly noted that *only* in virtue of sacred ordination does the work obtain that full, univocal meaning that tradition has attributed to it.[32]

---

[31] Instruction *Ecclesia de Mysterio*, August 15, 1997, Practical Provisions, Article 1, §1, "Need for an Appropriate Terminology", quoting John Paul II, Discourse at the Symposium on "The Participation of the Lay Faithful in the Ministry" (April 22, 1994), no. 3, *L'Osservatore Romano*, English language ed., May 11, 1994.

[32] Ibid., Article 1, §2, lightly emended.

It is necessary to be precise in using vocabulary.[33] Some customs on the level of terminology end up creating serious doctrinal misunderstandings. The theological principle must be clear: "A person is not a minister simply in performing a task, but through sacramental ordination."[34] Non-ordained ministries are not in themselves the fruit of a personal vocation, in other words, of a vocation to a state of life. They are services that each baptized person can render to the Church for a time.

However, as Joseph Ratzinger remarks:

> The Church, if she is deprived of spiritual vocations over a long period, might be tempted to create for herself a substitute clergy, so to speak, of purely human origin.... Yet if on that account the prayer for sacramental vocations were to take a back seat, if the Church, here and there, were to start being self-sufficient in that way and making herself independent of the gift of God, so to say, then she would of course be acting like Saul, who

---

[33] "The non-ordained faithful may be generically designated 'extraordinary ministers' when deputed by competent authority to discharge, solely by way of supply, those offices mentioned in Canon 230, § 3, and in Canons 943 and 1112. Naturally, the concrete term may be applied to those to whom functions are canonically entrusted, e.g., catechists, acolytes, lectors, etc. Temporary deputation for liturgical purposes—mentioned in Canon 230, § 2—does not confer any special or permanent title on the non-ordained faithful" (ibid., Article 1, §3).

[34] Instruction *Ecclesia de Mysterio*, Theological Principles, 2, "Unity and Diversity of Ministerial Functions".

when hard-pressed by the Philistines did indeed
wait a long time for Samuel but who, when he
did not appear and the people began running
away, lost patience and presented the burnt-
offering sacrifice himself. Since he had thought
he could hardly do otherwise in an emergency,
that he could and must take God's business into
his own hands, he was now told that by doing
that he had ruined his chances: to obey is better
than sacrifice (see 1 Sam 13:8–14; 15:22).[35]

The creation of lay "ministries" must therefore be
considered with great caution. We must be afraid
of taking God's place and organizing the Church
in a merely human manner. We must regain the
courage to persevere in prayer for vocations.

It is crucial to gauge the importance of priestly
celibacy so that the Church can understand herself. Effectiveness and organization, understood in
a purely human way, cannot govern our decisions.
We must learn to make room for the Holy Spirit
in our government and in our pastoral plans.

Confusion in understanding the priesthood

I would like to continue this study by emphasiz-
ing how the ordination of married men would

---

[35] Ratzinger, "Church Movements", in *Pilgrim Fellowship*, 181.

cause confusion and obscure the work that the Church has accomplished in promoting a better understanding of the priesthood.

What is an exception?

Someone might point out to me that there are exceptions already and that married men have been ordained priests in the Latin Church while continuing to live *more uxorio* [as married couples] with their wives. Yes, these are exceptions in the sense that these cases result from an uncommon situation that must not be induced to recur. So it is when married Protestant pastors enter into full communion [with the Catholic Church] and are to receive priestly ordination. An exception is by definition transitory, an incidental occurrence in the normal and natural state of affairs. That is not the case with a remote region that lacks priests. The shortage of them is not an exceptional state. This situation is common in all mission countries and even in the countries of the secularized West. By definition, a nascent Church lacks priests. The early Church found herself in this situation. We have seen that she did not renounce the principle of clerical continence. The ordination of married men, even if they were permanent deacons before, is not an exception but a rupture, a wound in the consistency of the priesthood. To speak of an exception would be a misuse of language or a lie.

The lack of priests could not justify such a rupture, because, once again, it is not an exceptional situation. Moreover, the ordination of married men in young Christian communities would prevent them from giving rise to priestly vocations of celibate priests. The exception would become a permanent state detrimental to the correct understanding of the priesthood.

Besides, the statement that the ordination of married men would be a solution given the shortage of priests is an illusion. Saint Paul VI already remarked: "We are not easily led to believe that the abolition of ecclesiastical celibacy would considerably increase the number of priestly vocations: the contemporary experience of those Churches and ecclesial communities which allow their ministers to marry seems to prove the contrary."[36]

The number of priests would not be increased significantly. Instead, the correct understanding of the priesthood and of the Church would be permanently confused as a result.

With a view to ordaining married men, some theologians have gone so far as to consider adapting the priesthood by reducing it to

---

[36] Paul VI, Encyclical *Sacerdotalis Caelibatus*, June 24, 1967, no. 49.

the administration of the sacraments alone. This proposal, which aims to separate the *tria munera* (three offices of sanctifying, teaching, governing), totally contradicts the teaching of Vatican Council II, which affirms their substantial unity (*Presbyterorum Ordinis*, nos. 4–6). This theologically absurd plan reveals a functionalist concept of the priesthood. With Benedict XVI, we have often wondered how one could hope for any more vocations from that perspective. What is to be said about the plan to have a married clergy side by side with a celibate clergy?[37] We run the risk of inculcating in the minds of the faithful the idea of a high and a low clergy.[38]

Eucharistic celibacy

The demand to ordain married men reveals a profound ignorance of the ontological bond between celibacy and priesthood. Western university

---

[37] See Fritz Lobinger, *Qui ordonner? Vers une nouvelle figure de prêtres* (Ixelles: Lumen Vitae, 2009).

[38] In 1873, the Ordinary of Bergamo, Bishop Pierluigi Speranza, wanted to make the transition from pastoral care by visitation to pastoral care of presence in the hamlets and small villages of the mountain region. He decided to provide them all with a resident priest from the local community. In about fifteen years, they ordained one hundred fifty mature men, widowers or celibates, after a rudimentary formation in a specific seminary. In 1888, they had to interrupt the experiment because the Christian people deeply despised these priests, most of whom did not hear confessions.

circles have sometimes spread a purely legal and disciplinary concept of celibacy. Some go so far as to say that celibacy is the distinguishing feature of religious life and should be reserved to it. John Paul II emphasized that "it is especially important that the priest understand the theological motivation of the Church's law on celibacy."[39]

Here I would like to address this theological foundation so as to draw from it several pastoral consequences. The nuptial meaning of celibacy that we have already mentioned must be elaborated. Indeed, priestly celibacy proceeds from a necessary Eucharistic nuptial character.[40]

Saint Paul VI suggested it in this way in 1967:

"Laid hold of by Christ" (Phil 3:12) unto the complete abandonment of one's entire self to Him, the priest takes on a closer likeness to Christ, even in the love with which the eternal Priest has loved the Church His Body and offered Himself entirely for her sake, in order to make her a glorious, holy and immaculate Spouse (Eph 5:25–27).

The consecrated celibacy of the sacred ministers actually manifests the virginal love of Christ for the Church, and the virginal and supernatural fecundity of this marriage.[41]

[39] John Paul II, *Pastores Dabo Vobis*, no. 29.

[40] See Laurent Touze, "Théologie du célibat sacerdotal", *Nova et Vetera* 94/2 (2019): 138–41.

[41] Paul VI, Encyclical *Sacerdotalis Caelibatus*, June 24, 1967, no. 26.

Christ offered himself on the altar of the Cross. Every day, the priest renews this oblation in pronouncing the words: "This is my Body, which will be given up for you." These words take on for him the meaning of entering into Christ's virginal offering. Every time a priest repeats "this is my Body", he offers his body, as a man, in continuity with the sacrifice on the Cross.

In a homily given on the occasion of my golden priestly Jubilee on September 28, 2019, I recalled: "A priest is a man who takes the place of God, a man who is vested with all the powers of God. See the power of the priest! The priest's tongue makes a God out of a piece of bread."[42] Now this miracle will not happen unless we agree to be crucified with Christ. Each one of us must agree to say with Saint Paul: "I have been crucified with Christ; it is no longer I who live, but Christ who lives in me; and the life I now live in the flesh I live by faith in the Son of God, who loved me and gave himself for me" (cf. Gal 2:20). Only through the Cross, at the conclusion of a prodigious descent into an abyss of humiliations, did the Son of God give to priests the divine power of the Eucharist. The innermost dynamism of the priest, the pillar on which his priestly existence is built,

---

[42] Saint John Vianney, quoted in Bernard Naudet, *Jean-Marie Vianney, curé d'Ars: Sa pensée, son coeur* (Paris: Cerf, 2007).

as Saint Josemaría Escrivá declared, is the Cross of
our Lord Jesus Christ. He proclaimed this in his
motto: "*In laetitia nulla dies sine cruce*": "In joy, no
day without the cross." Now the priest's joy is
experienced fully in the Holy Mass. It is the reason for his existence and gives meaning to his life.
At the altar, the priest stands beside the Host. Jesus
looks at him, and he looks at Jesus. Are we quite
conscious of what it means to have Christ himself
truly present before our eyes? In every Mass, the
priest finds himself face to face with Jesus. At that
time, the priest is identified with Christ, configured to him. He does not become only an *alter
Christus*, another Christ. He truly is *ipse Christus*;
he is Christ himself. He is clothed with the person of Christ himself, configured by a specific and
sacramental identification to the High Priest of
the Eternal Covenant (see *Ecclesia de Eucharistia*,
no. 29). Again Saint Josemaría Escrivá says: "We
priests, whether we are sinners or saints, are no
longer ourselves when we celebrate the Holy
Mass. We are Christ who renews on the altar the
divine sacrifice of Calvary."[43] Indeed, at the altar
I do not preside at this Mass that unites us. Jesus is
the one who presides at it in me. Although I am
unworthy of it, Jesus is truly present in the person

---

[43] Josemaría Escrivá, *Prêtre pour l'éternité* (Perenchies: Imprimerie D.
Decoster, 1983).

of the celebrant. I am Christ: what a terrifying statement! What a formidable responsibility! It is in his name and in his place that I stand at the altar (*Lumen Gentium*, no. 28). *In persona Christi* [in the person of Christ], I consecrate the bread and the wine, after having handed over to him my body, my voice, my poor heart so often soiled by many sins. On the eve of each Eucharistic celebration, if we remain like children snuggled in her arms, the Virgin Mary prepares us to deliver ourselves body and soul to Jesus Christ so that the miracle of the Eucharist might be accomplished. The Cross, the Eucharist, and the Virgin Mary fashion, structure, nourish, and consolidate our Christian and priestly life. You understand why every Christian, and, more particularly, the priest, must build his interior life on these three realities: *Crux, Hostia, et Virgo*. The Cross causes us to be born to divine life. Without the Eucharist, we cannot live. The Virgin, like a mother, watches attentively over our spiritual growth. She educates us to grow in faith. Jesus reveals to us the secret of this heavenly nourishment in which his own flesh becomes our food. We can live with his life in an unheard-of intimacy with him. The priest is truly the friend of Jesus. He offers himself to God. He offers himself to the whole Church and to each of the faithful to whom he is sent. The priest learns the logic of his celibacy in the Eucharist. "Acting in the person of Christ, the priest unites himself most intimately with the offering, and places on the altar his entire life, which bears the marks of the holocaust."[44] He learns in the Eucharistic sacrifice what the total gift of self means.

Priestly celibacy is born of the Eucharist. It gives a sacrificial meaning to the entire life of the priest. "It is from the Eucharist that he receives the grace and obligation to give his whole life a 'sacrificial' dimension."[45] The connection between continence and the Eucharistic celebration, which has always been perceived by the *sensus fidei* of the faithful, both in the West and in the East, therefore has nothing to do with a ritual taboo about sexuality. Rather, it is a profound insight into the "eucharistic form of the Christian life".[46]

Celibacy appears as the front door leading priests into this Eucharistic form. No one can

---

[44] Paul VI, Encyclical *Sacerdotalis Caelibatus*, no. 29.

[45] John Paul II, *Pastores Dabo Vobis*, no. 23.

[46] Benedict XVI, Post-Synodal Apostolic Exhortation *Sacramentum Caritatis*, February 22, 2007, no. 80. "In addition to its connection to priestly celibacy, the eucharistic mystery also has an intrinsic relationship to consecrated virginity, inasmuch as the latter is an expression of the Church's exclusive devotion to Christ, whom she accepts as her Bridegroom with a radical and fruitful fidelity. In the Eucharist, consecrated virginity finds inspiration and nourishment for its complete dedication to Christ. From the Eucharist, moreover, it draws encouragement and strength to be a sign, in our own times too, of God's gracious and fruitful love for humanity.... In this sense, it points to that eschatological horizon against which the choices and life decisions of every man and woman should be situated" (*Sacramentum Caritatis*, no. 81).

remain faithful to celibacy without the daily celebration of the Mass. In the Eucharist, the priest receives celibacy as a gift. We could sum up this connection between Eucharistic celebration and celibacy with the words of Marc Cardinal Ouellet: "Celibacy ... corresponds to the Eucharistic oblation of the Lord, who, out of love, gave his body once and for all, to the extreme point of distributing it sacramentally, and who demands of a man with a vocation a response of the same kind, in other words, total, irrevocable, and unconditional."[47] If Christ gives himself as food, then the priest, too, must be "a man who is crucified and eaten", as Blessed Antoine Chevrier put it. Celibacy is the sign of this and its concrete realization. I am firmly persuaded that the Christian people "recognize" their priests thanks to this sign. Through the instinct of faith, the faithful of all cultures unfailingly recognize Christ offered for all in the celibate priest.

Priestly celibacy and inculturation

Consequently, I would like to express my deep indignation when I hear it said that the ordination of married men is a necessity since the peoples of

---

[47] Marc Ouellet, *Celibato e legame nuziale di Cristo alla Chiesa* (Vatican City: Libreria Editrice Vaticana, 2016), 50.

Amazonia do not understand celibacy or that this reality will always be foreign to their culture. I see in this sort of argument a contemptuous, neo-colonialist, and infantilizing mentality that shocks me. All the peoples of the world are capable of understanding the Eucharistic logic of priestly celibacy. Are these peoples supposedly devoid of the instinct of the faith? Is it reasonable to think that God's grace would be inaccessible to the peoples of Amazonia and that God would deprive them of the grace of priestly celibacy that the Church has guarded for centuries as a precious jewel? There is no culture that God's grace cannot reach and transform. When God enters into a culture, he does not leave it intact. He destabilizes and purifies it. He transforms and divinizes it. Why would there be in the most remote areas of Amazonia more difficulties in understanding priestly celibacy? Let us not be afraid if celibacy goes against the local cultures. Jesus tells us: "I have not come to bring peace, but a sword" (Mt 10:34). The contact between the Gospel and a culture that is unacquainted with it is always disconcerting. The Jews and the Greeks of the first centuries were surprised, too, by celibacy for the Kingdom. It is a scandal for the world and will always remain so because it makes present the scandal of the Cross.

Some Western missionaries no longer understand the profound meaning of celibacy and project their doubts onto the Amazonian peoples. I would like to mention the enlightening testimony of a missionary who was present at the synod who knows the local situation well. Father Martin Lasarte organizes the forty-seven Salesian missionary communities of the region, which have in all 612,000 Christians belonging to sixty-two different ethnic groups.[48]

> In Latin America there is no lack of positive examples, such as among the Quetchi of central Guatemala (Verapaz) where, despite the absence of priests in some communities, lay ministers have living communities, rich in ministries, liturgies, catechetical itineraries, missions, among which the evangelical groups have been able to penetrate very little. Despite the scarcity of priests for all the communities, it is a local Church rich in indigenous priestly vocations, where even female and male religious congregations of totally local origin have been founded.
>
> Is the lack of vocations to the priesthood and religious life in the Amazon a pastoral challenge or is it rather the consequence of theological-pastoral options that have not given the expected results or only partial results? In my opinion, the proposal of the *viri probati* as a solution to evangelization is an illusory, almost magical proposal

---

[48] Study dated May 20, 2019, published on the official website of PIME, *Asia News*, on October 10–11, 2019.

that goes nowhere near to addressing the real underlying problem.

Father Lasarte cites also the example of some five hundred populations and ethnic groups that live around the Congo River. Christianity is sometimes considered the religion of the colonial power. Nevertheless, the flourishing of the African Churches is promising. Priestly vocations have increased by 32 percent over the last ten years, and the trend continues. Father Lasarte continues as follows:

> The inevitable question that arises is: how is it possible that peoples with so many anthropological-cultural riches and similarities with the Amazonian peoples, in their rituals, myths, a strong sense of community, communion with the cosmos, with profound religious openness ... have vibrant Christian communities and flourishing priestly vocations while in some parts of the Amazon, after 200, 400 years, there is ecclesial and vocational sterility? There are dioceses and congregations which have been present for over a century yet do not have a single local indigenous vocation.[49]

In every region of the world, Christian communities encounter trials and difficulties, but

[49] Ibid, lightly emended.

evidence shows that wherever there is a serious, authentic, and continual evangelization activity, there is no lack of priestly vocations.

Along these lines, Pope Francis boldly affirms with lucidity and courage:

> Many places are experiencing a dearth of vocations to the priesthood and consecrated life. This is often due to a lack of contagious apostolic fervor in communities which results in a cooling of enthusiasm and attractiveness. Wherever there is life, fervor and a desire to bring Christ to others, genuine vocations will arise.... [T]he fraternal life and fervor of the community can awaken in the young a desire to consecrate themselves completely to God and to the preaching of the Gospel. This is particularly true if such a living community prays insistently for vocations and courageously proposes to its young people the path of special consecration.[50]

The pope points out the basis for the problem: a lack of faith and of apostolic fervor. They have stopped proclaiming Christ. I am convinced that if we offer evangelization work to young people, the number of missionary vocations will rise.

Alas, under the pretext of inculturation, wrongly understood, Catholics often are content

---

[50] Pope Francis, Apostolic Exhortation *Evangelii Gaudium*, November 24, 2013, no. 107.

to defend the rights of the indigenous peoples or to work to promote their economic development. This is not the heart of the mandate that Jesus gave us. He told us: "Go therefore and make disciples of all nations, baptizing them in the name of the Father and of the Son and of the Holy Spirit, teaching them to observe all that I have commanded you" (Mt 28:19–20). Thus we take great care of the indigenous populations, but not enough to proclaim to them the heart of our faith. I am ashamed to admit it, but the Evangelical Protestants are sometimes more faithful to Christ than we are. We have become specialists in the fields of social, political, or economic activity. Nevertheless, as Benedict XVI reminded us, "The faithful expect only one thing from priests: that they be specialists in promoting the encounter between man and God."[51]

Pope Francis very clearly explained this problem in his speech at the closing of the synod. He mentioned the necessary renewal of missionary zeal. He recalled very clearly that evangelization is the heart of the synodal reflection: what is at stake is the proclamation of salvation in Jesus Christ. And so, in order to respond to his appeal, by priestly celibacy "we want to go ahead and

[51] Benedict XVI, Address to the Polish clergy, Warsaw Cathedral, May 25, 2006.

make present this scandal of a faith that bases all existence on God."[52] In a new surge of evangelization, we want to make present through celibacy what the world does not want to see: God alone suffices. He alone can save us and make us fully happy.

Toward a radically evangelical priesthood

The priesthood is going through a crisis. Detestable scandals have disfigured its face and unsettled many priests throughout the world. Now within the Church, crises are always overcome by returning to the radical character of the Gospel, and not by adopting worldly criteria.

Celibacy is a scandal for the world. We are tempted to tone it down. On the contrary, Saint John Paul II maintained that it is necessary to rediscover that

> the Spirit, by consecrating the priest and configuring him to Jesus Christ, head and shepherd, creates a bond which, located in the priest's very being, demands to be assimilated and lived out in a personal, free and conscious way through an ever richer communion of life and love and an ever broader and more radical sharing in the

---

[52] Benedict XVI, Vigil on Saint Peter's Square, Dialogue with Priests, June 10, 2010.

feelings and attitudes of Jesus Christ. In this bond between the Lord Jesus and the priest, an ontological and psychological bond, a sacramental and moral bond, is the foundation and likewise the power for that "life according to the Spirit" and that "radicalism of the Gospel" to which every priest is called.[53]

We will not solve the crisis of the priesthood by weakening celibacy. On the contrary, I am convinced that the future of the priesthood lies in Gospel radicalism. Priests must live out celibacy and a kind of poverty. They are called to it in a special way. Celibacy, poverty, and fraternity lived out in obedience by priests are not only means of personal sanctification; they become signs and instruments of a specifically priestly life: "The priest is called to live these evangelical counsels in accordance with those ways and, more specifically, those goals and that basic meaning which derive from and express his own priestly identity."[54] The logic of disappropriation resulting from celibacy must go so far as obedience and the renunciation of property in poverty. Benedict XVI states this forcefully: "Without such a forsaking on our part there is no priesthood. The call to follow Jesus is not possible without this

---

[53] John Paul II, *Pastores Dabo Vobis*, no. 72.
[54] Ibid., no. 27, lightly emended.

sign of freedom and renunciation of any kind of compromise."[55]

The full concept of priesthood includes a life led according to the evangelical counsels. I think that it is time for bishops to take concrete steps to propose this "fully priestly" life to their priests, a common life in prayer, poverty, celibacy, and obedience. The more priests live the radical character of the Gospel, the more consistent their identity and their everyday life will be. There is a work of reform to undertake here, in other words, a return to the sources. I am not confusing priestly life and religious life.[56] I solemnly declare that the priesthood is a state of life that involves an existence given and consecrated in truth.

A life led according to the world can produce in a priestly soul only a feeling of inconsistency, incompleteness, and being torn apart. "No one can serve two masters" (Mt 6:24).

Dear brother priests, allow me to address you directly. Sexual scandals erupt at a regular pace.

[55] Joseph Cardinal Ratzinger, *Journey to Easter*, trans. Dame Mary Groves (1987; New York: Crossroad, 2005), 155, lightly emended.

[56] The priestly state by its nature does not require the profession of the evangelical counsels but, rather, a life led according to the counsels. It is up to religious men and women to be consecrated by their state of life through the profession of the vows with a view to becoming prophetic signs of the radical character of the Gospel in the Church. (See Vatican Council II, Dogmatic Constitution on the Church *Lumen Gentium*, November 21, 1964, no. 44; Pius XII, Allocution *Annus Sacer*, December 8, 1950.)

They are broadcast far and wide by the social networks. They cover us with shame because they directly call into question our promise of celibacy in imitation of Christ. How can we bear the fact that some of our brothers could profane the sacred innocence of children? How could we hope for any missionary fruitfulness if such atrocities are committed in secret? Some of you are crushed by work. Others celebrate in empty churches. I wish to remind all of you: the experience of the Cross reveals the truth of our life. In proclaiming God's truth, you get onto the Cross. Without you, humanity would be less great and less beautiful. You are the living rampart of the truth because you agreed to love it even to the Cross. You are not the defenders of an abstract or partisan truth. You have decided to suffer for love of Jesus Christ. All of you, hidden and forgotten priests, you whom society sometimes despises, you who are faithful to the promises of your ordination, you cause the powers of this world to tremble. You remind them that nothing can resist the force of the gift of your life for the sake of truth. Your presence is unbearable to the prince of lies.

Celibacy reveals the very essence of the Christian priesthood. To speak about it as an accessory reality is hurtful to all the priests in the world. I am firmly convinced that relativizing priestly celibacy is tantamount to reducing the priesthood to a mere function. Now, the priesthood is not a function, but a state of life.

The priestly vocation: a vocation to prayer

Dear brother priests, dear seminarians who are preparing for the priesthood, I know that many of you suffer terribly to see celibacy criticized and despised. I know how lonely you feel and how abandoned by those from whom you expect support. Do not let yourselves be troubled by these petty, vain, and pitiful theological opinions of the moment. If you come to doubt your vocation or are tempted to retreat, given the demands of celibacy, meditate on these brilliant, forceful words by Benedict XVI:

> [Jesus] supports us. Let us fix our gaze ever anew on him and reach out to him. Let us allow his hand to take ours, and then we will not sink....
>
> One of my favorite prayers is the request that the liturgy puts on our lips before Communion: "... never let me be separated from you." Let us ask that we never fall away from communion with his Body, with Christ himself, that we do not fall away from the Eucharistic mystery. Let us ask that he will never let go of our hands....
>
> The Lord laid his hand upon us. He expressed the meaning of this gesture in these words: "No

longer do I call you servants, for the servant does not know what his master is doing; but I have called you friends, for all that I have heard from my Father I have made known to you" (Jn 15:15).

I no longer call you servants but friends: in these words one could actually perceive the institution of the priesthood. The Lord makes us his friends; he entrusts everything to us; he entrusts himself to us, so that we can speak in his name, *in persona Christi capitis*.

What trust! He has truly delivered himself into our hands.... I no longer call you servants but friends. This is the profound meaning of being a priest: becoming the friend of Jesus Christ. For this friendship we must daily recommit ourselves.... We must put into practice this communion of thought with Jesus, as St. Paul tells us in his Letter to the Philippians (cf. 2:2–5). And this communion of thought is not a purely intellectual thing, but a sharing of sentiments and will, hence, also of actions. This means that we should know Jesus in an increasingly personal way, listening to him, living together with him, staying with him.

Listening to him—in *lectio divina*, that is, reading Sacred Scripture in a non-academic but spiritual way; thus, we learn to encounter Jesus present, who speaks to us. We must reason and reflect, before him and with him, on his words and actions. The reading of Sacred Scripture

is prayer, it must be prayer—it must emerge
from prayer and lead to prayer.

The Evangelists tell us that the Lord frequently withdrew—for entire nights—"to the
mountains", to pray alone. We too need these
"mountains": they are inner peaks that we must
scale, the mountain of prayer.

Only in this way does the friendship develop.
Only in this way can we carry out our priestly
service, only in this way can we take Christ and
his Gospel to men and women.

Activism by itself can even be heroic, but in
the end external action is fruitless and loses its
effectiveness unless it is born from deep inner
communion with Christ. The time we spend on
this is truly a time of pastoral activity, authentic
pastoral activity. The priest must above all be a
man of prayer.

The world in its frenetic activism often loses
its direction. Its action and capacities become
destructive if they lack the power of prayer,
from which flow the waters of life that irrigate
the arid land.

I no longer call you servants, but friends. The
core of the priesthood is being friends of Jesus
Christ. Only in this way can we truly speak *in
persona Christi*, even if our inner remoteness from
Christ cannot jeopardize the validity of the Sacrament. Being a friend of Jesus, being a priest,
means being a man of prayer. In this way we
recognize him and emerge from the ignorance

of simple servants. We thus learn to live, suffer and act with him and for him.

Being friends with Jesus is always friendship with his followers. We can be friends of Jesus only in communion with the whole of Christ, with the Head and with the Body; in the vigorous vine of the Church to which the Lord gives life....

I would like to end this Homily with a word on Andrea Santoro, the priest from the Diocese of Rome who was assassinated in Trebizond while he was praying.... [Fr. Santoro said:] "I am here to dwell among these people and enable Jesus to do so by lending him my flesh.... One becomes capable of salvation only by offering one's own flesh. The evil in the world must be borne and the pain shared, assimilating it into one's own flesh as did Jesus."

Jesus assumed our flesh; let us give him our own. In this way he can come into the world and transform it.[57]

The Mass is the priest's reason for existing. The renewal of the Sacrifice of Calvary is not only the most important and the loftiest action of his day, but the one that confers all its meaning on it. The saintly Curé of Ars often repeated with tears in his eyes: "Ah! How terrifying it is to be a priest!" Then he would add: "How sad it is when a priest

[57] Benedict XVI, Homily, April 13, 2006.

celebrates Mass as though it were an ordinary thing. How far astray a priest without an interior life has wandered!"[58]

Dear priests, dear seminarians, let us not allow ourselves get caught up in haste, activism, and the superficiality of a life that gives priority to social or ecological commitment, as though time dedicated to Christ in silence were lost time. It is precisely in prayer and adoration in front of the tabernacle that we find the indispensable support for our virginity and our priestly celibacy.

Let us not become discouraged: prayer demands an effort. It involves a kind of hand to hand combat, an arduous struggle with God, like that of Jacob, who wrestled the whole night until the dawn (Gen 32:22–32). Sometimes we get that painful impression that Jesus is being silent, because he is working in the utmost secrecy. Let us be diligent in our prayer of adoration, and let us teach it to the Christian faithful by the example of our lives. In order to encourage priests to have an intimate relation with the Lord, Saint Charles Borromeo always used to say: "You will not be able to care for the souls of others if you let your own perish. In the end you will no longer do anything even for others. You must always have time for being with God."[59]

[58] Naudet, *Jean-Marie Vianney*, 1014–18.
[59] Quoted in Benedict XVI, Meeting with the Clergy of the Diocese of Bolzano-Bressanone, August 6, 2008.

Are you exercising the care of souls? ... Do not thereby neglect yourself. Do not give yourself to others to such an extent that nothing is left of yourself for yourself. You should certainly keep in mind the souls whose pastor you are, but without forgetting yourself. My brothers, do not forget that there is nothing so necessary to all churchmen than the meditation which precedes, accompanies and follows all our actions: I will sing, says the prophet, and I will meditate (cf. Ps 100:1). If you administer the sacraments, my brother, meditate upon what you are doing. If you celebrate Mass, meditate on what you are offering. If you recite the psalms in choir, meditate to whom and of what you are speaking. If you are guiding souls, meditate in whose blood they have been cleansed.[60]

Saint John Paul II commented as follows on the invaluable advice of Charles Borromeo to priests:

The priest's prayer life in particular needs to be continually "reformed". Experience teaches that in prayer one cannot live off past gains. Every day we need not only to renew our external fidelity to times of prayer, especially those devoted to the celebration of the Liturgy of the Hours and those left to personal choice and not reinforced by fixed times of liturgical service, but also to strive

---

[60] Saint Charles Borromeo, *Acta Ecclesiae Mediolanensis* (Milan, 1599), 1178; quoted in John Paul II, *Pastores Dabo Vobis*, no. 72.

constantly for the experience of a genuine personal encounter with Jesus, a trusting dialogue with the Father and a deep experience of the Spirit.

What the apostle Paul says of all Christians, that they must attain "to mature manhood, to the measure of the stature of the fullness of Christ" (Eph 4:13), can be applied specifically to priests, who are called to the perfection of charity and therefore to holiness, even more so because their pastoral ministry itself demands that they be living models for all the faithful.[61]

Dear priests and seminarians, given the widespread religious indifference and the crisis of doctrine, if you want your faith to remain strong and vigorous, it is advisable to nourish it with a diligent, humble, and confident prayer life. Persevere and keep being models and masters of prayer:

> May your days be marked by times of prayer, during which, after Jesus' example, you engage in a regenerating conversation with the Father. I know it is not easy to stay faithful to this daily appointment with the Lord, especially today when the pace of life is frenetic and worries absorb us more and more. Yet we must convince ourselves: the time he spends in prayer is the most important time in a priest's life, in which divine grace acts with greater effectiveness, making his

[61] John Paul II, *Pastores Dabo Vobis*, no. 72.

ministry fruitful. The first service to render to the community is prayer. And therefore, time for prayer must be given a true priority in our life.[62]

Build your existence on the firm framework of a plan of life. Ask the Lord constantly to unify your life. Work and prayer do not turn their backs on each other, far from it; they must support one another. If we are not interiorly in communion with God, we can give nothing to others. We must constantly rediscover that God is our priority. Benedict XVI said: "To be ordained priests means to enter in a sacramental and existential way into Christ's prayer for 'his own'. From this we priests derive a particular vocation to pray.... The priest who prays a lot, and who prays well, is progressively drawn out of himself and evermore united to Jesus the Good Shepherd and the Servant of the Brethren."[63] Without faith and prayer, priestly celibacy would be like a house built on sand; it collapses when the storm comes. Without prayer and a lively faith, how could we understand priestly celibacy and live it joyfully?

Dear brother priests and bishops, let us reread the profound words by Benedict XVI:

[62] Benedict XVI, To the clergy of the Archdiocese of Brindisi, June 15, 2008.
[63] Benedict XVI, Homily for the Ordination to the Priesthood of 19 Deacons of the Diocese of Rome, May 3, 2009.

Paul calls Timothy—and in him, the Bishop and in general the priest—"man of God" (1 Tim 6:11). This is the central task of the priest: to bring God to men and women. Of course, he can only do this if he himself comes from God, if he lives *with* and *by* God.... The true foundation of the priest's life, the ground of his existence, the ground of his life, is God himself.

The Church ... has rightly seen in the following of the Apostles, in communion with Jesus himself,... the explanation of what the priestly mission means. The priest can and must also say today, with the Levite: "*Dominus pars hereditatis meae et calicis mei.*" God himself is my portion of land, the external and internal foundation of my existence.

This theocentricity of the priestly existence is truly necessary in our entirely function-oriented world in which everything is based on calculable and ascertainable performance. The priest must truly know God from within and thus bring him to men and women: this is the prime service that contemporary humanity needs. If this centrality of God in a priest's life is lost, little by little the zeal in his actions is lost. In an excess of external things the center that gives meaning to all things and leads them back to unity is missing. There, the foundation of life, the "earth" upon which all this can stand and prosper, is missing.[64]

---

[64] Benedict XVI, Address to the Roman Curia, December 22, 2006.

This teaching is the charter for all reform, for all renewal of the priesthood in the Catholic Church. It definitively clarifies the meaning and the necessity of celibacy. The priest can and must have nothing but God. He must be poor in all things except God. He must manifest by his way of life that God is at the center of all evangelization and of all pastoral work.

Celibacy, in force for Bishops throughout the Eastern and Western Church and, according to a tradition that dates back to an epoch close to that of the Apostles, for priests in general in the Latin Church, can only be understood and lived if it is based on this basic structure.

The solely pragmatic reasons, the reference to greater availability, is not enough: such a greater availability of time could easily become also a form of egoism that saves a person from the sacrifices and efforts demanded by the reciprocal acceptance and forbearance in matrimony; thus, it could lead to a spiritual impoverishment or to hardening of the heart.

The true foundation of celibacy can be contained in the phrase: *Dominus pars*—You are my land. It can only be theocentric. It cannot mean being deprived of love, but must mean letting oneself be consumed by passion for God and subsequently, thanks to a more intimate way of being with him, to serve men and women, too. Celibacy must be a witness to faith: faith in God materializes in that form of life which only has meaning if it is based on God.

Basing one's life on him, renouncing marriage and the family, means that I accept and experience God as a reality and that I can therefore bring him to men and women. Our world, which has become totally positivistic, in which God appears at best as a hypothesis but not as a concrete reality, needs to rest on God in the most concrete and radical way possible.

It needs a witness to God that lies in the decision to welcome God as a land where one finds one's own existence. For this reason, celibacy is so important today, in our contemporary world, even if its fulfilment in our age is constantly threatened and questioned.

A careful preparation during the journey towards this goal and persevering guidance on the part of the Bishop, priest friends and lay people who sustain this priestly witness together, is essential. We need prayer that invokes God without respite as the Living God and relies on him in times of confusion as well as in times of joy. Consequently, as opposed to the cultural trend that seeks to convince us that we are not capable of making such decisions, this witness can be lived and in this way, in our world, can reinstate God as reality.[65]

Our world needs priestly celibacy more than ever. It is necessary for priests, but also indispensable

[65] Ibid.

from a pastoral perspective. It has a burning missionary relevance.

In conclusion, let us review the essential foundations of what we have said. Christ Jesus is a priest. His whole being is priestly, dedicated, and handed over. Before him, priests offered to God animals in sacrifice. He revealed to us that the true priest offers himself. From now on, in order to be a priest, we must enter into this great offering of Christ to the Father. We must adopt the sacrifice of the Cross as the form of our whole life.

This gift takes the form of the sacrifice of the husband for his wife. Christ is truly the Bridegroom of the Church. The priest, in turn, hands himself over for the whole Church. Celibacy manifests this gift; it is the concrete, vital sign of it. Celibacy is the seal of the Cross on our lives as priests. It is a cry of the priestly soul that proclaims love for the Father and the gift of oneself to the Church.

The priest is capable of being a husband and a father according to the flesh, but by his celibacy he renounces that form of human flourishing. Out of love, he chooses to deprive himself of it in order to live as the exclusive husband of the Church. The intention to relativize celibacy is tantamount to contempt for this radical gift that so many faithful priests have lived out since their ordination.

Celibacy is the sign and instrument of our entrance into the priestly being of Jesus. It takes on a value that we could describe analogically as sacramental. From this perspective, we do not see how the priestly identity could be encouraged and protected if in one region or another they suppressed the requirement of celibacy as Christ intended it and as the Latin Church has jealously preserved it.

As Vatican Council II recalls, clerical celibacy is not a mere precept of the ecclesiastical law[66] but, rather, a "precious gift" from God.[67] This is why Pope Francis, adopting as his own the resolute and courageous words of Saint Paul VI, says: " 'I would rather give my life than change the law on celibacy.' ... Personally, I think that celibacy is a gift for the Church. Second, I don't agree with allowing optional celibacy, no."[68]

There is an ontological-sacramental connection between priesthood and celibacy. To diminish this connection in any way would be to call into question the Magisterium of the council and of Popes Paul VI, John Paul II, and Benedict XVI. I humbly beg Pope Francis to protect us from such a possibility by vetoing any attempt to weaken the law of priestly celibacy, even limited to one particular region.

---

[66] John Paul II, *Pastores Dabo Vobis*, no. 50.

[67] Vatican II, *Presbyterorum Ordinis*, no. 16.

[68] Pope Francis, Press conference on the return flight from World Youth Day in Panama, January 27, 2019.

To conclude this text, I would like to turn once again to my dear brother priests. Christ left to us an enormous and magnificent responsibility. We continue his presence on earth. Like him, we must watch, pray, and be steadfast in the faith.

He was willing to have need of us priests. Our hands consecrated by the sacred chrism are no longer ours. They are his in order to bless, forgive, and console. They are reserved to him. If sometimes celibacy seems to us too burdensome, let us look at the hands of the Crucified. Our hands, like his, must be pierced so as to keep and to hold nothing greedily. Our heart, like his, must be open so that everyone finds welcome and refuge there. Therefore, if we no longer understand our own celibacy, let us look at the Cross. It is the only book that will give us the true meaning of it.

Only the Cross will teach us to be a priest. Only the Cross will teach us to "love to the end" (cf. Jn 13:1). On this path, Benedict XVI is an admirable model.

Robert Cardinal Sarah
Vatican City, November 25, 2019

In the Shadow of the Cross

Conclusion by the Two Authors

The priesthood is going through a dark time. Wounded by the revelation of so many scandals, disconcerted by the constant questioning of their consecrated celibacy, many priests are tempted by the thought of giving up and abandoning everything.

Christ asks us: "Will you also go away?" (Jn 6:67). United to Peter and to his successor, we intend to answer him: "Lord, to whom shall we go? You have the words of eternal life" (Jn 6:68).

Yes, Lord, you are the Holy One of God. You are the Consecrated One of God. You offered everything and gave everything. Your "yes" to the Father is unconditional. Nothing in you resists it; nothing in you escapes it. We priests want to follow you even to this perfect "yes". We want to say with you: here is my body given up for you; here is my blood that will be poured out for you and for the multitude. Teach us to pray and to repeat continually after you: "Into your hands I commit my spirit" (Lk 23:46). You are our only good, our only inheritance.

With Saint John Henry Newman, we pray to you:

Possess my whole being so utterly that my life may only be a radiance of Thine. Shine through me and be so in me that every soul I come in contact with may feel Thy presence in my soul. Let them look up and see no longer me but only Thee, O Lord! Stay with me and then I shall begin to shine as Thou shinest, so to shine as to be a light to others. The light, O Jesus, will be all from Thee; none of it will be mine. It will be Thou who shinest through me upon others. O let me thus praise Thee in the way Thou dost love best, by shining on all those around me. Let me preach Thee without preaching, not by words but by example, by the catching force, the sympathetic influence of what I do, the evident fullness of the love which my heart bears to Thee.

Jesus Crucified, look upon your Church as you looked at Mary from the top of the Cross. You gave her as a mother to John, the chaste priest and apostle. You entrusted her to him so that she might become "his own" (Jn 19:27). Have mercy on your Church. Give her peace and unity. Have mercy on your priests. Grant that they may welcome Mary in turn. Grant that they may have no other good than your Church.

Jesus Crucified, look at the Church your Bride. Make her beautiful and worthy of you. May she be conformed to your Heart. May everyone be able to recognize your face in her. May all peoples recognize in her at last their sole common home.

Having arrived at the end of our reflection, we feel the necessity of professing our love for the Church. We have tried to give her our life, as Christ offered his for her. We will never abandon her. We wear on our right hand the ring that reminds us that we are bound to her in a definitive covenant.

Every day our soul gives thanks for and marvels at this unmerited gift that has been given to us of serving and loving the Church. Confronted with this mystery, we exclaim with Saint Augustine: "O sacrament of piety, O sign of unity, O bond of charity! The one who wants to live has somewhere to live, has something to live on. Let him approach, let him believe, let him belong to the body so as to be given life. Let him not shudder at the make-up of its members."[1] We want to remain aloof from everything that could harm the unity of the Church. Personal quarrels, political maneuvering, power plays, ideological manipulations, and critiques full of bitterness play the game of the devil—the divider, the father of lies.

Our decision to take up a pen and write for you was prompted solely by our love for the Church.

The words of Saint Paul resound like a solemn warning for all bishops:

[1] Saint Augustine, *In Iohannis Evangelium*, 26, 13. English translation from: *The Works of Saint Augustine*, vol. I/12, *Homilies on the Gospel of John 1–40* (Hyde Park, N.Y.: New City Press, 2009), 461.

> I charge you in the presence of God and of Christ Jesus who is to judge the living and the dead ...: preach the word, be urgent in season and out of season, convince, rebuke, and exhort, be unfailing in patience and in teaching. For the time is coming when people will not endure sound teaching, but having itching ears they will accumulate for themselves teachers to suit their own likings, and will turn away from listening to the truth and wander into myths. (2 Tim 4:1–4)

We are living through these difficult, troubled times in distress and suffering. It was our sacred duty to recall the truth about the Catholic priesthood. For through it, the whole beauty of the Church is being called into question. The Church is not a human organization. She is a mystery. She is the Mystical Bride of Christ. Our priestly celibacy continually reminds the world of precisely this.

It is urgent and necessary for everyone— bishops, priests, and lay people—to stop letting themselves be intimidated by the wrong-headed pleas, the theatrical productions, the diabolical lies, and the fashionable errors that try to devalue down priestly celibacy.

It is urgent and necessary for everyone— bishops, priests, and lay people—to take a fresh look with the eyes of faith at the Church and at priestly celibacy, which protects her mystery.

This fresh look will be the best rampart against the spirit of division, against the spirit of politics, but also against the spirit of indifference and relativism.

Let us listen to Saint Paul. Let us speak up boldly to profess the faith without fear of being uncharitable. In these difficult times, everyone should fear to hear God say to him someday "these acerbic words by way of reprimand": "Accursed are you who said nothing. Ah! Enough silence! Cry out in a thousand tongues. I see that by dint of silence the world has been corrupted, the Bride of Christ is quite pale; she has lost her color, because they are sucking her blood, the blood of Christ which is given by grace.... Stop sleeping the sleep of negligence. Do what you can promptly."[2]

What is to be done? In the first place, we must listen anew to God's call: "You shall be holy; for I the LORD your God am holy" (Lev 19:2). Priestly ordination leads to identification with Christ. Certainly, the substantial effectiveness of the ministry remains independent of the minster's holiness, but we cannot ignore, either, the extraordinary fruitfulness produced by the holiness of priests.

---

[2] Saint Catherine of Siena, Letter no. 16 [84], *À un grand prélat* ["To a great prelate"].

No one is prevented from proclaiming the truth of the faith in a spirit of peace, unity, and charity. Woe to the one who remains silent. "*Vae mihi si non evangelizavero!*" "Woe to me if I do not preach the gospel!" (1 Cor 9:16).

Text written by Cardinal Sarah,
read and approved by Benedict XVI.
Vatican City, September, 2019